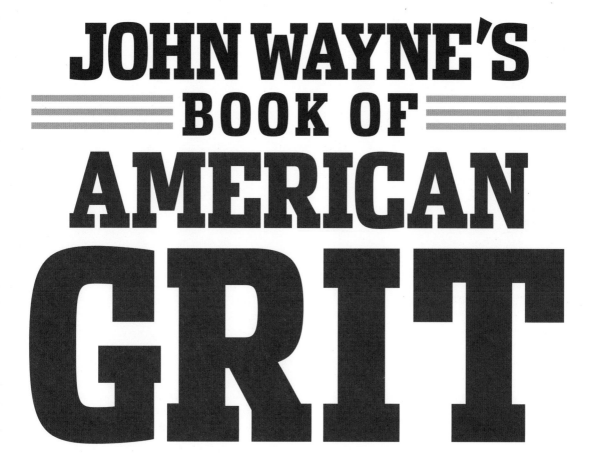

JOHN WAYNE'S
BOOK OF
AMERICAN
GRIT

John Wayne

Amelia Earhart

Thomas Edison

4

FOREWORD

A welcome from Ethan Wayne

6

TENACITY

The ones who persisted

46

INGENUITY

Inspiration
meets perspiration

CONTENTS ★

Nellie Bly   Jackie Robinson   Tammy Duckworth

86
RESILIENCE
Those who never quit

126
COURAGE
The bold and the brave

166
SACRIFICE
All gave some, some gave all

MY FATHER UNDERSTOOD AMERICA HAS ALWAYS BEEN A COUNTRY OF RUGGED INDIVIDUALISTS.

It's a land whose enduring freedoms were forged through sweat, smarts and sheer will. It's why he was drawn to playing timeless trailblazers—some of whom were inspired directly by our country's history—because there's no need to embellish when it comes to true grit. Whether he was Davy Crockett looking to fight for Texas independence, Lt. Col. Benjamin Vandervoort leading his men during the D-Day landings, or Frank "Spig" Wead serving in combat after learning to walk again, Duke wanted to highlight our country's real-life heroes whenever he could. I know he'd be proud of this collection of 125 American leaders, icons and pioneers whose legendary tenacity, ingenuity, resilience, courage and sacrifice exemplify what makes our nation, and her people, so great.

—Ethan Wayne

Duke means business in a scene from *True Grit* (1969).

★ TENACITY ★

WHETHER YOU'RE SHOOTING FOR THE MOON
OR HANGING ON FOR ALL YOU'VE GOT, IT TAKES
TRUE GRIT TO KEEP MOVING FORWARD.

John Wayne in *The Man Who Shot Liberty Valance* (1962). The Duke character Tom Doniphon embodies the kind of tenacity John Wayne would show later in the 1960s when he performed some of his own stunts after having most of a lung removed in a cancer operation.

BECOMING
★ JOHN WAYNE ★

LOSING A SCHOLARSHIP TURNED INTO DUKE'S FIRST STEP ON THE ROAD TO FAME BECAUSE OF HIS TIRELESS REFUSAL TO LET A BAD BREAK SLOW HIM DOWN.

THOUGH HE'S WIDELY regarded as one of the greatest actors of his generation, John Wayne didn't grow up with dreams of gracing the silver screen. In fact, long before John Wayne blew audiences away by spin-cocking a Winchester rifle in the 1939 film *Stagecoach*, he had been on the fast track to becoming a college football player. While matriculating at the University of Southern California, Duke was an up-and-coming starting tackle who owed his enrollment to the coveted football scholarship he'd earned as a standout at Glendale Union High School.

But during his sophomore year, while body surfing at Newport Beach, Duke sustained a serious injury, an accident made all the more painful when it cost him his scholarship. Without the funds necessary to continue pursuing his degree, a destitute Duke was forced to leave the team. An earlier rejection letter from the U.S. Naval Academy added insult to injury, and with limited prospects, Duke found himself in desperate need of a job. Aware of his former player's dire financial troubles, USC coach Howard Jones got in touch with an old pal making waves in Hollywood and helped Duke get his foot in the door as a hardworking propman, setting him on the course of a whole new career.

As he hauled set pieces around bustling studio backlots, Duke slowly warmed to the increasingly appealing notion of becoming an actor. To achieve this, however, he would spend the next few years accepting an array of bit parts and unbilled roles in films by such studios as Metro-Goldwyn-Mayer, First National Pictures, Warner Bros. and Fox Film Corporation. For a Hollywood hopeful like Duke, taking on these gigs was a great way to network, but he couldn't have known just how richly his efforts would pay off.

The future Oscar winner's silver screen debut came with a somewhat ironic twist: Fresh off his failed undergraduate career, the 19-year-old got the chance to fulfill his dreams of college football glory by briefly appearing as an uncredited football player in MGM'S 1926 sports film *Brown of Harvard*. (He reprised the role of a pigskin-tossing athlete again in the 1927 football drama *The Drop Kick*.) Shortly after, Duke took a walk-on role as an extra in 1926's *The Great K & A Train Robbery*, his first of many Westerns, and in just three years, the busier-than-ever propman worked his way to earning an onscreen credit as "Duke Morrison" in the 1929 early talkie *Words and Music*. In another amusing twist of fate, Duke vicariously lived out his goal of joining the U.S. Naval Academy by playing a midshipman in *Salute* (1929), a movie about two brothers divided by college football rivalry in the Army-Navy Game. Directed by John Ford, Duke's contributions to *Salute* included assisting the costume designer and finally delivering his first line of dialogue: "He doesn't mean the audience. What do the actors do, Mister?"

At 23, Duke snagged the starring role in Fox's 1930 Western *The Big Trail*. Although he had spent years diligently paying his dues around various film sets across town, Duke largely owed this fortuitous turn of events to the intervention of John Ford. When director Raoul Walsh approached Ford about casting a fitting lead for Fox's ambitious new project, Ford recommended the hardworking propman with whom he'd maintained a friendly rapport.

Walsh took a massive gamble by picking the relatively unknown Duke, and while the director was confident his young star's natural talent would be enough to portray the film's protagonist, other studio heads were less than impressed. Some executives saw the fresh-faced Duke as a liability—historically, casting an unfamiliar newcomer in the lead role didn't bode well for ticket sales. The publicity department rushed to justify their newest leading man, and where many stars of the era were given hyped or wholly fabricated backstories to promote an extra-marketable air of mystery, sex appeal or refinement, Duke's studio-scripted biography stayed close to the truth. Notably missing: any mention of his birth name, Marion Morrison, which was considered ill-befitting of a tough-talking Western star. Instead, *The Big Trail* saw Duke officially introduced to the public as John Wayne.

Released in 1930 at a then-staggering cost of about $2 million, the epic adventure featured John Wayne as Breck Coleman, a man who leads hundreds of families in wagon trains to resettle way out West. Shot in an ambitious 70mm "Grandeur" format, the film was doomed from the start; most theaters lacked the equipment to show widescreen features, and the stock market crash ensured they wouldn't make the upgrades, which meant a majority of moviegoers missed out on the film's gorgeous sweeping vistas and were instead treated to a heavily-edited 35mm edition. Through no fault of his own, Duke's Oregon Trail flick almost ended his career before it began.

But John Wayne persevered. After *The Big Trail*'s disappointing box office returns, Duke committed himself to finding more work—any work—as an actor. Determined to make a lasting name for himself, the actor dramatically upped the ante on his acting output, appearing in more than 60 films between October 1930 and February 1939 (in 1933 alone, Duke added his name to a whopping 11 films). While sticking to a series of low budget B-Westerns, the would-be leading man showed a willingness to perform in any capacity, playing everything

Duke as Breck Coleman in *The Big Trail* (1930).

from a corpse in 1931's *The Deceiver* to a naïve conquest of Barbara Stanwyck's sex-crazed, social climbing heroine in *Baby Face* (1933). In 1937, Duke rose to the challenge of learning how to skate in order to embody a convincing pro hockey player in the sports drama *Idol of the Crowds*; given that he was raised in California, this proved to be no easy task. Nonetheless, as with every other acting endeavor, John Wayne stayed the course.

By the time John Ford cast him in 1939's *Stagecoach*, Duke was ready to give the director his all. Nine years after his career was announced DOA, with just one spin of a Winchester rifle, John Wayne emerged triumphant from the B-films of his youth as the larger-than-life gunslinging icon of the American West. His story shows that with enough tenacity, even the most monumental failures can be turned into an opportunity for growth.

★ TEDDY ROOSEVELT ★

BEFORE MAKING STRIDES as a "Rough Rider" charging up Kettle Hill, Theodore Roosevelt's formative years got off to a rough start. The future 26th president suffered from debilitating asthma attacks as a child, which left him feeling like he was being smothered to death. Rather than let his physical limitations keep him down, Roosevelt conditioned his frail young body through vigorous exercise and plenty of fresh air, forming healthy habits he'd turn to for the rest of his life.

After graduating from Harvard, Roosevelt launched a career in politics and married his first love, Alice Hathaway Lee; sadly, these halcyon days would not last. Just two days after giving birth to their first child—four years to the day after their engagement—the young Mrs. Roosevelt died from Bright's disease. Adding to this tragedy, his mother passed away only hours before her daughter-in-law. He marked the loss of the two most important women in his life with one poignant, devastating journal entry: a bold, black "X" followed by the words, "The light has gone out of my life."

Reeling with grief, Roosevelt left his infant daughter in his sister's care and struck out for the Dakota Territories. After two years working as a rancher (and losing his herd of cattle to a particularly cold winter), he emerged from the wilderness, setting his sights on fighting the scourge of corruption plaguing his hometown. Armed with renewed purpose, Roosevelt returned to New York City, married a childhood friend and reunited with his daughter. The feisty Republican politician leapt up the ladder and made a name for himself with astounding speed: from NYC Police Commissioner to Governor of New York to the office of vice president, even making time to fight in the Spanish-American War. When President William McKinley took two bullets in the abdomen and died, Roosevelt found himself sworn in as the youngest Commander-in-Chief in our nation's history.

With no vice president appointed during his first term, Roosevelt first shouldered the weight of the Oval Office alone. Over the course of two terms, he passed legislation establishing five national parks, strengthened the U.S. Navy, spearheaded the construction of the Panama Canal, received a Nobel Peace Prize for helping end the Russo-Japanese War and more before leaving office in 1909.

Finding his former protégé, the newly-elected President William Howard Taft, "unfit for leadership" in the highest office of the land, Roosevelt saddled up for one last ride on the 1912 campaign trail. While addressing a crowd in Milwaukee, Wisconsin, the former president found himself on the business end of a disgruntled saloonkeeper's gun—fortunately, the bullet first struck Roosevelt's steel glasses case and a 50-page copy of his speech. After correctly deducing the shot was not fatal, Roosevelt spoke for another 90 minutes, finishing his speech before agreeing to accept first aid. The "Bull Moose" carried the evidence of his close call for the rest of his life. As a real-life prototype of the persona John Wayne embodied on the big screen, Roosevelt proved that with enough gumption, you can will yourself through any stretch of wilderness—literal or figurative—and come out stronger than ever.

Duke made sure Davy Crockett's signature coonskin cap was featured in the film.

John Wayne starred as Davy Crockett in *The Alamo* (1960), a film which he also directed and produced. Duke felt so strongly about telling this story he financed much of it himself, making this movie one of the most intensely personal projects of his entire career.

THIS LARGER-THAN-LIFE Tennessean knew what it meant to stand up and fight, no matter the cost. Davy Crockett got his start herding cattle, hunting and telling stories along the way, endearing himself to the citizens of his home state. After serving three terms as a member of the House of Representatives, Crockett left Tennessee to travel west with a group of well-armed volunteers to support the Provisional Government of Texas in their fight against Gen. Santa Anna. Outmanned and outgunned, the final battle to defend the Alamo lasted almost 90 minutes, and by the bloody end, the famous frontiersman had been slain. While no one knows exactly how he died, one thing's for certain: Davy Crockett had no desire to surrender. A true hero of the frontier days, his sacrifice—as well as that of the rest of Tennesee's volunteers—will live on everytime we remember the Alamo.

★ DEBORAH SAMPSON ★

DURING A TIME when women were expected to be nurses or, more often, stay home, Deborah Sampson chose to fight instead. At 21, the most famous woman to have fought in the Revolutionary War donned men's clothes, bound her chest and enlisted as a man in an Army unit. During her first battle, two musket balls hit her in the thigh. Rather than risk a doctor blowing her cover, Deborah took matters into her own hands and dug one out with a penknife. The other stayed embedded in her leg until her death. She continued to fight under the guise of her donned masculinity for nearly a year and a half. Over the course of her service to her country only one doctor discovered her secret; mercifully, he kept it to himself.

at the end of the war, having lived to fight another day and giving new meaning to the

★ VINCE LOMBARDI ★

EVERY YEAR THE Super Bowl Champions raise the Lombardi Trophy, the most coveted accolade in their game, after winning the most important game of the season. In doing so they honor the legacy of a man widely considered to be the greatest football coach of all time, Vince Lombardi. But Lombardi wasn't chosen as the namesake for the most significant trophy in the game he loved because of tactical prowess alone: Lombardi was a shining example of the steadfast dedication to hard work and doing the right thing that makes for a rare kind of tenacity.

Born in the Sheepshead Bay area of Brooklyn, New York, in 1913, Lombardi's young adulthood was, like Duke's, colored by the harsh realities of the Great Depression. The oldest of five children, Lombardi was studying for the priesthood at the Cathedral College of Immaculate Conception in Queens when the stock market crashed. By 1932, the realities of Depression-era New York made Lombardi give up his spiritual studies in favor of a traditional curriculum. At St. Francis Prep, also in Queens, Lombardi was an academic standout, earning admission to Fordham University, and also made a name for himself as fullback on the football team.

It would be this latter pursuit, at first a hobby, that would eventually grow into a passion so consuming for Lombardi that despite forays into law and finance, he found himself coming back to the game again and again. Finally, he took a job as a teacher and football coach at St. Cecilia High School in Englewood, New Jersey. Eight years later, he had proven

such a versatile tactician on the gridiron that Fordham once again came calling, this time to offer Lombardi a job on its coaching staff. A coaching stint at West Point followed, where he stood out for his relentless work ethic. Among those who noticed were the New York Giants, who soon took a chance on the college veteran by hiring him as their offensive coordinator.

When the Giants won the 1956 Championship, Lombardi's stock was as high as it had ever been, and he was ready to take the reigns as a head coach. In 1959, nearly two decades after football had presented itself as an outlet for this hardworking son of Italian immigrants, Lombardi took the job that would make him a household name, signing a five-year contract with the Green Bay Packers. Lombardi's strategy was based on the same values that saw him work his way to the apex of his craft. He understood that when something is executed perfectly after hours of practice, it doesn't have to be fancy to be effective. In an era when interests from the Jim Crow South still controlled football's discussions on race, he scoffed at the idea that skin color should determine who qualified to be a Packer. It was the work that mattered.

He believed in that doctrine and expected it from his players. During his tenure, the Packers became the most successful franchise of the 1960s, winning five NFL championships including the first two to be dubbed the "Super Bowl," in which the NFL and the American Football League faced off against one another to determine which league reigned supreme. Lombardi rose to the challenge, leading his Packers to victory over the Kansas City Chiefs in that first Super Bowl, and the rest is history.

★ RAY CHARLES ★

ONG BEFORE he became known for pioneering the soul genre, Ray Charles used music to escape the hellish nightmares of his youth. Raised in poverty by a single mother, Charles witnessed his younger brother drown, a memory that haunted him long after he lost his vision. By enrolling at a school for the blind, the future superstar found a place where he could develop his budding talents by learning to read music in braille. When his beloved mother died, the newly-orphaned prodigy left school and hit the road, accompanying and arranging music for bands in cities from Miami to Seattle. Charles's unique blend of gospel and R&B managed to bring black and white audiences together even at the height of segregation. "Brother Ray" overcame a significant visual impairment, senseless prejudice and a battle with addiction to become one of our nation's most beloved performers. Want proof? The state of Georgia adopted its talented native son's number, "Georgia On My Mind," as the official state song.

★ MICKEY MANTLE ★

O AMOUNT OF physical pain could stop Mickey Mantle from batting his way into Hall of Fame glory. As a high school athlete, one well-placed kick to the shin nearly cost him a career in sports (and his leg) after he developed a serious bone infection. He fully recovered, and by 19, Mantle had worked his way through the minor leagues and landed a coveted spot on the New York Yankees. After tearing his ACL in 1951, "The Mick" played every game for the rest of his career in excruciating pain but kept swinging for the fences—the 16-time All-Star racked up seven

The Wright brothers' first flight on December 17, 1903.

Top: Orville Wright
Bottom: Wilbur Wright

ORVILLE AND
★ WILBUR WRIGHT ★

AS CHILDREN, Orville and Wilbur Wright first dreamt of defying gravity after receiving a toy helicopter from their father. Though they'd opened a bicycle shop to capitalize on the recent cycling trend, their attention was always turned toward the sky. For seven years, the Wrights studied the design of gliders and closely watched birds in flight, enduring failure after failure in a quest to design a working flying machine. Their unrelenting determination finally paid off in 1903 when Orville, riding aboard their aptly named Wright Flyer, soared through the air for a total of 12 seconds. Mocked or otherwise ignored by the press at home and abroad, the brothers refused to listen to the naysayers and took their flying machine to Europe, demonstrating their new technology to rave reviews—a testament to believing in yourself and the loftiness of your dreams.

★ JIMMY CARTER ★

PRIOR TO PAVING the way for the Camp David accords, Jimmy Carter got his first taste of the value of hard work on a humble peanut farm. The future 39th president grew up in the aftermath of the Great Depression in the poverty-stricken small town of Archery, Georgia, and although his father was a staunch segregationist, the elder Carter allowed his son to play with their young African American neighbors. As a teenager, Carter aspired to serve his country in the U.S. Naval Academy, a dream that came to fruition after the U.S. entered World War II. While studying at the Academy, Carter met and fell in love with a friend of his sister, Rosalynn Smith, beginning a romance that persists to this day.

After serving aboard the USS *Pomfret* and USS *Barracuda*, the naval officer confronted the dangers of nuclear energy head-on when he was sent to shut down a failed nuclear reactor at the Chalk River Laboratories in Canada. Leading a team of Americans and Canadians in a race to contain the threat, Carter donned protective gear, braved radioactive water and descended into the heart of the reactor to disassemble its ruined core, all in 90-second intervals. This harrowing mission, which left his body radioactive for months afterward, would later shape his nuclear nonproliferation policies as president.

Carter's ambition to work aboard a nuclear submarine came to a halt when he was called home to manage the family peanut farm in the wake of his father's passing. While this proved a difficult change of pace for his growing family, Carter turned the chance to return to his roots into a vehicle for growth.

While living in public housing, the budding agribusinessman put his technical know-how and resolve to the test—when drought knocked out the first year's harvest, he and Rosalynn persevered, keeping the farm afloat. With racial tensions at an all-time high during the era of *Brown v. Board of Education*, the hardworking, accountable Carter championed the merits of integration, winning a seat in Georgia's Senate in 1963 followed by a bid for Governor of Georgia in 1970.

Owing perhaps in part to the friendships of his youth, the young governor refused to kowtow to the demands of the Ku Klux Klan—rather, he displayed portraits of Martin Luther King Jr. and other esteemed African American Georgians in the state capitol building while the Klan protested outside. In 1976, Carter ran for the presidency and won, putting his family peanut farm into a trust to avoid conflicts of interest. Over the course of his term in office, he fostered the negotiation of peace agreements between Egypt and Israel, established the U.S. Department of Energy and Department of Education and even maintained a correspondence with John Wayne despite their political differences, and posthumously awarded Duke the Presidential Medal of Freedom.

In his later years, Carter has devoted himself to philanthropic work, creating the Carter Center—a nonprofit organization which, among other endeavors, has led efforts to eradicate the Guinea worm disease—winning the Nobel Peace Prize and building houses for families in need with Habitat for Humanity. His lifetime of service to the public shows that real heroes will do what is necessary to get the job done right.

★ OPRAH WINFREY ★

HEN MOST PEOPLE think of Oprah Winfrey, the television talk show queen and media powerhouse extraordinaire, the image of a teenager faced with an unexpected pregnancy is probably the furthest thing that comes to mind. But that's exactly how the astounding brilliance of Oprah's success first took shape: in her triumph over a youth marked by unfathomable trauma.

Born "Orpah" to a teenage mother in rural Mississippi, Oprah spent her earliest years living in her impoverished grandmother Hattie Mae's care. She wore dresses made from potato sacks to school, where classmates teased her tattered clothes. At church services with Hattie Mae, the young girl developed a love for reading and public speaking. After several years, a 6-year-old Oprah reunited with her mother, Vernita Lee, who settled the family in a Milwaukee, Wisconsin slum; later, she was sent to live with her father, Vernon, in Nashville, Tennessee, where she further developed her public speaking skills at various church engagements. These happy years in Nashville came to an end, however, when Vernita Lee arranged for her firstborn to return to Milwaukee.

When Oprah was 9, three different members of her family took advantage of her, subjecting her to abuse. Unable to process what had happened, Oprah began acting out and skipping school. Pushed to her limits and no longer willing to cope with her child's recklessness, Vernita Lee sent her daughter packing back to Nashville. At just 14 years old, Oprah discovered she was pregnant and delivered a baby boy who died weeks later.

Emotionally shattered, the teenager resolved to turn her life around. She threw herself into achieving high marks in her high school studies, becoming an honors student and earning a college scholarship. A part-time job at a radio station led to full-time employment, and by 19, Oprah was the youngest (and first African American woman) news anchor at Nashville's WTVF-TV.

In her late twenties, Oprah had worked her way from Nashville to Baltimore to Chicago, where she became the host of the WLS-TV half-hour morning talk show *AM Chicago*. In a matter of months, her personality, presence and charm endeared her to viewers, making *AM Chicago* the highest rated talk show in the city. Impressed by her success, legendary film critic Roger Ebert convinced her to syndicate the program, which was renamed *The Oprah Winfrey Show*. Now accessible to a nationwide audience, she quickly perfected her heartfelt, confession-style approach to the traditional talk show format. Through confronting tough topics, such as her own abuse, she inspired others to do the same and begin their own healing processes. As an example, she made waves in 1987 by speaking with racist, homophobic residents of Forsyth, Georgia, seeking to understand the root of their hatred while maintaining her composure.

Outside of her wildly popular show, which ran for a whopping total of 25 seasons, Oprah's accolades also include receiving the Presidential Medal of Freedom and creating her own television network, the Oprah Winfrey Network (OWN). She is living, breathing proof that by never giving up, we can achieve more than the sum of all our wildest dreams.

★ FRANK "SPIG" WEAD ★

John Wayne portrayed the legendary aviator Frank Wead in *The Wings of Eagles* (1957). A former naval officer himself, John Ford had been a close friend of Wead's, and chose to direct the film as a way to honor Wead's accomplishments as well as the U.S. Navy.

The script for Wead's story was approved by the Pentagon and the U.S. Navy Office of Information.

BORN TO A FAMILY of war veterans going back several generations, Frank Wead overcame incredible odds in pursuit of an extraordinary life. Wead stuck to tradition while still carving his own path by joining the Armed Forces as a Naval aviator. A quick learner, Spig, as he was called, shattered records for seaplane racing. Unfortunately, while home on leave in 1926, tragedy struck the up-and-coming aviator when he took a serious fall down a staircase and fractured his neck. This horrific accident effectively ensured his immediate retirement from flying. Never one to quit, Wead didn't let his physical limitations get him down and willed himself to walk again in just two years. Drawing on his flying experiences for reference, he spent his time writing screenplays for Hollywood, including films such as *Test Pilot, Midshipman Jack* and *20,000 Men a Year.*

After hearing reports about the Japanese attack on Pearl Harbor, Wead insisted on being allowed to return to active duty with the Navy and served aboard the USS *Essex*. Wead was also credited with developing the use of escort carriers, a smaller auxiliary force that would follow the main fleet. Also called "jeep escorts," escort carriers were cheap to manufacture, easy to build and could still carry planes like aircraft carriers, making them extremely useful in terms of quickly mobilizing troops. In a pinch, they could serve as emergency airstrips as well as provide cover for larger carriers. John Wayne helped bring Wead's story to life by playing the aviator turned screenwriter in John Ford's *The Wings of Eagles* (1957).

★ TRAVIS KAUFFMAN ★

FOR MOST PEOPLE, fighting like your life depends on it usually involves facing life's challenges in a metaphorical way. Not Travis Kauffman. He saved his own skin by wrestling a mountain lion with his bare hands.

While training for an upcoming race, the 31-year-old outdoors enthusiast heard pine needles rustling on the path behind him. He turned to see a young mountain lion trailing him by mere feet. The deadly predator pounced, sinking its teeth into Kauffman's right wrist, its claws slashing his shoulder and legs. Kauffman mustered his strength to throw the animal off of him. Its jaw still grinding away at his wrist, he pushed through the excruciating pain, and when blunt objects failed to stop the creature, he stood on its neck. Fearing its mother would suddenly appear and leap to her offspring's defense, Kauffman steeled himself to finish the fight. After several heart-pounding minutes, the cat's body thrashed, then relaxed. He had managed to suffocate it with his body weight. Covered in scratches and cuts, Kauffman pried his arm free and ran the three miles back to the beginning of the trail before being taken to a hospital.

Twenty stitches in his cheek, nose and wrist later, Kauffman survived his harrowing ordeal in one piece. And while the gutsy outdoorsman certainly didn't wake up planning to prove his drive to survive that day, his close call with a big cat shows that where there's a will, there's a way.

DUKE ★ KAHANAMOKU ★

BORN DUKE PAOA Kahinu Mokoe Hulikohola Kahanamoku to native Hawaiian parents in 1890, the future father of surfing was only a toddler when pineapple magnate Sanford Dole, backed by U.S. forces, mounted a successful coup d'état to overthrow the Kingdom of Hawaii. In its place he established a republic, and in 1898, the U.S. officially annexed Hawaii (it would not become an official state until 1959). This swift and troubling takeover profoundly disturbed the collective psyche of native Hawaiians. Robbed of their sovereignty, the islanders felt their traditional ways of life were more at risk of disappearing than ever before. After enduring two centuries of visits from potential colonizers, losing control over their land proved an unfamiliar burden to bear.

Surfing, an ancient Hawaiian activity which foreign missionaries had attempted to ban, was still practiced by those brave souls who dared to ride the waves. Drawn to the sea, Kahanamoku learned how to surf at 8 years old, beginning a lifelong love and dedication to the sport. This turn to traditional culture gave the young swimmer a sense of identity he could cling to in the midst of overwhelming change.

After spending his younger years developing his wave riding prowess, by his early twenties, Kahanamoku qualified for the Olympics. At the 1912 Summer Olympics in Stockholm, Sweden, Duke became the first Hawaiian to win an Olympic medal by taking home the gold and silver in the 100-meter freestyle and the men's 4x200-meter freestyle relay respectively. Kahanamoku racked up two gold medals in the 1920 Olympics and a silver medal in the 1924 games (his brother won the bronze).

On June 14, 1925, a vessel capsized outside Newport Harbor in Newport Beach, California. Living there at the time, Kahanamoku grabbed his board and hit the surf, swimming to the site of the wrecked ship and loading all the survivors he could fit on his surfboard.

During World War II, he served with distinction as an MP in Hawaii and in 1948 he joined another Duke, the one and only John Wayne, in the film the *Wake of the Red Witch*. Kahanamoku later became the first inductee in both the Surfing and Swimming halls of fame. By honoring and furthering the traditions of his people at a time when more and more Hawaiians were Americanizing, the man Hawaiians knew as "The Duke" showed the Mainland 48 what a valuable addition to the U.S. the Hawaiian people and their culture were.

John Wayne and Duke Kahanamoku on the set of *Wake of the Red Witch* (1948). The surf legend and Olympic medalist plays a tribal chief named Ua Nuke in the film, which was shot on location at the Arboretum in Arcadia, California.

★ JOHN MUIR ★

WHILE IT'S TRUE that President Theodore Roosevelt established our country's National Park System, he couldn't have done so without the help of wilderness-loving Scottish-American conservationist John Muir. The future "Father of the National Park System" escaped his harsh religious upbringing by finding spirituality in nature, and spent his youth studying the flora and fauna he encountered while exploring swamps, streams, lakes and mountains throughout America.

In March 1867, Muir was working at a wagon wheel factory when a filing tool slipped out of his hand and lodged squarely in his right eye. While he cried out in agony, his left eye sympathetically failed, and in mere seconds, Muir's world plunged into darkness. But when his vision miraculously returned to his left eye weeks later, Muir resolved to spend as much time in the wilderness as possible.

That fall, with a crude map and little money in his pocket, Muir set off from Kentucky on a 1,000-mile solo trek to Florida. He slept under bushes and largely depended on the kindness of strangers for food and lodging, especially when he contracted malaria while hiking through swamps along the way. More adventures followed, including hiking from the Sierra Nevadas to Alaskan glaciers to exploring the Yosemite Valley. He began writing about the stunning beauty he observed along his travels, and of the need to protect these wild spaces from land development. He also witnessed farmers overgrazing their cattle, the felling of far too many trees with dynamite, out-of-control forest fires and other devastating man-made disasters wrought upon the environment out of ignorance and greed.

Something had to be done, so in 1889, Muir created a plan to preserve 1,200 pristine square miles of the Yosemite

Valley and protect it from mining and logging operations. Congress approved it the following year, and Yosemite National Park was born.

In a scene that could have been written into a Duke-starring biopic, in 1903, the conservationist invited Teddy Roosevelt to go camping. After the two rode horses, visited the towering granite monolith El Capitan and slept under giant sequoias, Roosevelt saw Muir's mission of land preservation to fruition, creating a total of five national parks. More than a century after his death, Muir's efforts made it possible for generations of Americans to enjoy the natural beauty of their land.

★ JIM THORPE ★

N 1911, THE CARLISLE Indian Industrial School was not the kind of school where Team USA expected to find its Olympic stars. Nor did professional baseball leagues, nor the NFL. But the humble school, a meager attempt at making amends for the injustices visited on native tribes throughout U.S. history, is exactly where one of America's finest athletes was produced. Taking the field against Harvard that year, Jim Thorpe, a 6'1" back from the Sac and Fox Nation, led Carlisle to victory by scoring four field goals, sealing the game at 18–15.

Thorpe, who would go on to play football and baseball professionally, was such an incomparable athlete that he found ways to achieve greatness even when the odds were against him. At the 1912 Olympics, Thorpe would win gold in the decathlon despite the fact that his running shoes had been stolen. (According to sporting legend, he made do with a discarded pair he'd found in the trash.) But arguably the most impressive story about Thorpe from that decathlon is his qualifying heat in the javelin throw. Not realizing he could take a running start, Thorpe threw the javelin from a standing position and still placed second. He was the first Native American to win Olympic gold, but draconian rules governing amateurism would soon

see those medals taken away—because Thorpe had played semi-pro baseball, he was deemed ineligible as an Olympian. But Thorpe never stopped chasing his passion, going on to play professional baseball and football and even living to see his life story made into the 1951 feature film *Jim Thorpe—All American*, starring Duke's friend Burt Lancaster. Thorpe carved out a career for himself as an unstoppable force on the gridiron, leaving behind a legacy as one of our country's greatest athletes.

★ SHIRLEY CHISHOLM ★

"FIGHTING SHIRLEY CHISHOLM" didn't want to be remembered as the first African American woman elected to Congress. All that mattered to her was being, in her words, "a catalyst for change in America."

Born to Caribbean immigrants in Brooklyn, New York, Chisholm and her three sisters grew up during the Great Depression, learning to make do with little and work hard for everything else. After being sent to primary school in Barbados, Chisholm discovered her aptitude for learning, viewing it as both a way to advance herself and help others. As a teenager, she returned home to Brooklyn and won numerous college scholarships before deciding to attend Brooklyn College, later receiving a Masters degree in early childhood education in 1951.

Working as a teacher and a consultant for child care centers in and around lower Manhattan whet Chisholm's appetite for politics as a means to better the lives of her disadvantaged neighbors. By the time she turned 40, Chisholm had been elected to New York's State Assembly; in 1968, she ran for a newly drawn election district in Brooklyn. Entering the race without having the support of the local Democratic party behind her, which she proudly called out in her slogan, "Unbought and Unbossed," Chisholm's fluency in Spanish helped her appeal to the diverse voters in her district, giving her an edge over the competition. After the last votes had been counted, it was clear: Chisholm triumphed over her Republican-backed opponent, civil rights activist James Farmer, by a two-to-one margin, becoming the first African American congresswoman.

Before Chisholm could crusade for higher wages for working class Americans or fight for educational reform, however, she reached a dead end in the form of the Agriculture Committee, where she could hardly do much good for her urban constituents. Annoyed, Chisholm filed a complaint, stating her wish to help the many veterans in her district. The bold move made waves, as newcomers were expected to accept their initial committee without fuss, but Shirley Chisholm was nobody's yes-woman. She moved to the Veteran's Affairs Committee, later working her way up the ladder to the Education and Labor and Rules Committees.

On January 25, 1972, Chisholm launched her boldest campaign yet: a run for the presidency, saying, "I stand before you today, to repudiate the ridiculous notion that the American people will not vote for qualified candidates, simply because he is not white or because she is not a male." In Raleigh, North Carolina, vandals covered her campaign materials with racist epithets.

When one of her rivals, the pro-segregation Governor of Alabama, George Wallace, was shot, Chisholm stunned both her fans and critics by visiting him in the hospital. Over the coming months, though, without the proper funds to achieve a large-scale campaign, she bowed out of the race. Years later, when Chisholm needed support for legislation to provide domestic workers with a minimum wage, Wallace convinced enough Southern congressmen to pass the bill in the House. Chisholm showed Americans that women of color could stand shoulder-to-shoulder with any other member in government.

★ MUHAMMAD ALI ★

CASSIUS MARCELLUS CLAY, Jr., the boy who would one day become Muhammad Ali, was born on January 17, 1942, in Kentucky's Louisville General Hospital. As a toddler, the overactive future champ took to dancing around the house on his tiptoes, and in school, he ran alongside the school bus rather than riding in it.

Upon discovering his new red bicycle had been stolen, an incensed 12-year-old Clay reported its theft to a police officer, saying how much he'd love to "whup" the thief responsible. The officer, Joe Martin, happened to be a boxing coach, and warned Clay to learn a thing or two about fighting before making threats. Clay began studying the finer points of boxing with Martin, and within six years the teenager brought home the gold at the 1960 Olympic games. During this time, after a period of soul searching, he converted to Islam and took the name Muhammad Ali.

As a professional, Ali became arguably the greatest boxer of all time, proving his fearlessness both in and out of the ring. He fought his way to multiple titles and was on the winning side of some of the most memorable bouts in history. But as the nation entered the Vietnam War, Ali felt called to defend something greater than a title: his conscience. In 1967, at the height of his athletic ability, the boxing champion refused to be drafted on religious and moral grounds, unable to reconcile serving his country with the racism he'd long faced as an African American in the South. Arrested and charged with draft evasion, he was sentenced to five years in prison and fined $10,000. Worst of all, his boxing license was revoked. Stripped of his titles, Ali wasn't sure when or if he would ever return to the ring. But before long, public opinion turned against the war, and by 1971, the U.S. Supreme Court

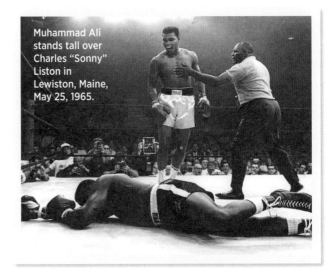

Muhammad Ali stands tall over Charles "Sonny" Liston in Lewiston, Maine, May 25, 1965.

overturned Ali's conviction, and he resumed his fighting career with renewed vigor, famously defeating the likes of Joe Frazier and George Foreman.

Even when he was no longer in his physical prime, Ali reminded the world exactly how courageous he was. Battling Parkinson's disease, an ailment that would eventually claim his life, Ali's hands trembled but his gaze was steady as he defiantly lit the torch at the 1996 Olympic Games—proving once again that he will always be "The Greatest."

DWAYNE "THE ROCK"
★ JOHNSON ★

 UKE AND THE ROCK have a lot in common. Both men started their adulthoods as football stars for some of the biggest programs in the country, USC and the University of Miami. Both had their dreams of gridiron glory dashed by injury and made their way into the entertainment industry. Both were physically imposing men who found a home in B-movies before working their way up to being among the highest-paid actors in the world—with their own production companies to boot. And both were able to achieve everything they did because of a stubborn refusal to stop moving forward.

Dwayne Johnson was born on May 2, 1972, to Ata Maivia Johnson and Rocky Johnson. His father and maternal grandfather were star professional wrestlers, and after Johnson's football career ended, he turned to the family business. For decades, he has electrified audiences as The Rock, a professional wrestling persona he still returns to from time to time. His dedication as a businessman—in addition to his production company, he is also heavily involved in other ventures, including his own tequila brand—is matched only by his dedication to his craft. He has been known to travel with his own full gym, setting up a complete complement of weights in tents on movie sets and vacation properties so that he can work out even when he's taking time off. It's a work ethic Duke would have admired.

THE "UNSINKABLE"
★ MOLLY BROWN ★

TODAY, MARGARET "MOLLY" Brown is most remembered for surviving the unthinkable when the so-called "unsinkable" *Titanic* met an icy end on its maiden voyage across the Atlantic. But beyond the disaster, Brown's indefatigable spirit and passion for helping those less fortunate buoyed her throughout her life and made her a true legend.

Born in 1867 to Irish immigrants, young Molly got a first-rate education in the hard realities of life by working long hours for meager pay at a factory. As a young adult, she moved to Leadville, Colorado, a town filled with people whose desire to strike it rich mining for gold left many of them broken and financially destitute. Seeing these frequently immigrant laborers endure backbreaking work while struggling to survive struck a chord with Brown, and soon she began volunteering in soup kitchens in order to lend a hand where she could.

At 19, she married a miner named J.J. "Jim" Brown and started a family. When Jim struck gold, the Browns became millionaires overnight. Despite her newfound financial stability, Brown remained committed to her philanthropic efforts. By 1909, the couple had separated, leaving her with a tidy cash settlement. Free to live however she pleased, Brown embarked on a tour of Egypt with fellow millionaire John Jacob Astor IV. But when word came that her eldest grandson was gravely ill back home in Denver, Brown immediately booked passage on the *Titanic* to sail home straight away.

At 11:40 p.m. on April 14, 1912, the *Titanic* scraped along an iceberg and water began pouring into its hull. After learning the ship would sink, rather than rush to save herself, Brown spent crucial minutes loading others into lifeboats. She rallied the other women to row and worked to keep everyone's spirits up despite the protests of Quartermaster Robert Hitchens, who ignored her demands to rescue the hundreds of people drowning before their eyes. Fed up with his lack of gumption, she threatened to throw him overboard, grabbed an oar and tried steering the boat toward the wreckage herself.

By 4 a.m., the *Carpathia* had arrived and began rescuing the *Titanic's* survivors. But by the time the ship docked in New York, Brown had already organized and been selected to lead the newly-formed Survivor's Committee as well as raised $10,000 to distribute to families in need. She steadfastly refused to disembark until all of the *Titanic* passengers aboard had made contact with their loved ones or received medical treatment.

Despite being excluded from giving testimony at the *Titanic* Senate inquiry due to her gender, Brown awarded the *Carpathia's* crew medals for their bravery. She traveled to Halifax, the final resting place for many of *Titanic's* victims, to place wreaths on their graves, helped erect a *Titanic* Memorial in Washington, D.C., and continued her work on the Survivor's Committee. Her tenacity in the face of tragedy ensured many people affected by the *Titanic* disaster would have the means necessary to pick up the pieces of their lives and move on.

DOUGLAS ★ MACARTHUR ★

General Douglas MacArthur (center) wades ashore at Leyte, Philippine Islands, on October 20, 1944.

DURING WORLD WAR II, General Douglas MacArthur saved countless lives in the South Pacific by leading a daring campaign to retake the Philippines from Japanese forces. The Supreme Commander of the Allied Forces in the Southwest Pacific Area had the pleasure of receiving the terms of Japan's unconditional surrender and, when many soldiers returned stateside, stayed behind to help the shell shocked nation re-establish order.

But MacArthur's finest hour came at the invasion of Inchon during the Korean War. Just two months after invading South Korea, the North Korean army had driven the Allies back to the southeast reaches of the Korean peninsula, pinning them against the sea.

Looking to regain a strategic advantage over the enemy, the Commander in Chief of the United Nations Command hedged his bets on a risky maneuver to draw attention away from the situation in the south.

On the morning of September 15, 1950, MacArthur ordered his troops to begin an amphibious assault on the coastal city of Inchon. Facing bad weather and an extreme high tide of more than 30 feet, a force of Marines overtook the harbor with little to no resistance, securing the beachhead in less than 24 hours. The troops began their push deep behind enemy lines, cutting off North Korean supplies and liberating the city of Seoul in just 10 days. By taking the enemy by surprise, MacArthur's bold vision turned the tide of the war in South Korea's favor.

BENJAMIN OLIVER
★ DAVIS JR. ★

IN HIS FIGHT against the Axis powers, Benjamin Oliver Davis Jr. struggled with the prejudices that had plagued his father throughout his military service. By 1941, the captain had experienced more than his share of racism in the United States armed forces. At West Point, the son of America's first African American Army general lived through four years of silent treatment hazing from his white classmates. He'd been turned away from the all-white Army Air Corps. While stationed at Fort Benning, he was banned from entering the officers' clubs. In fact, he'd been given the exact same runaround as his father when, rather than being allowed to command troops, he was sent to teach military tactics at the Tuskegee Institute. But that year, the War Department established the first black flying unit, and suddenly Davis found himself training for air combat with other African Americans.

These Tuskegee Airmen knew senior officials were watching their every move, ready to pounce on the slightest error. With Davis in command, the 99th Pursuit Squadron took to the skies over Tunisia and Sicily, providing air support to the Allied forces on the ground. Right as things were beginning to heat up, the colonel was called back stateside—top brass had gone behind his back and accused his men of underperforming. With his pilots still downing German planes left and right, Davis held a press conference at the Pentagon and defended his men before a War Department inquiry. Eventually, officials found the pilots of the 99th had performed as well as their white peers.

By the end of the war, Davis's men had shot down a total of 111 German planes, and Davis earned the Silver Star and the Distinguished Flying Cross for missions over Austria and Germany. When President Truman signed an executive order to enforce the racial integration of the armed forces, Col. Davis himself helped create the plan for integrating the Air Force

★ HELEN KELLER ★ AND ANNE SULLIVAN

UNABLE TO SEE, hear or speak, Helen Keller spent several years of her childhood effectively shut out from experiencing the fullness of the world, living as though she were drifting "at sea in a dense fog." But after a brilliant, patient teacher opened her eyes to the joy of language, Helen's insatiable drive to not only express herself but champion the rights of differently-abled people made her an inspirational phenomenon across the globe.

While she wasn't born deaf or blind in 1880, an illness when she was not quite 2 years old—likely scarlet fever or meningitis—robbed Helen of her sight, hearing and speech. Without the ability to communicate with those around her, the young child began acting out by hitting people, throwing tantrums, bursting into tears and more. While some thought these antics signaled a need to be institutionalized, Mr. and Mrs. Keller sought the advice of Alexander Graham Bell, who specialized in educating the deaf. At his suggestion, they inquired at the Perkins Institution for the Blind, and Anne Sullivan, a teacher who herself was an alumna of the school, was sent to Alabama to begin working one-on-one with Helen.

For their first meeting, Anne brought the precocious girl a doll, but before Helen could run off with the gift, Anne grabbed Helen's hand and spelled "d-o-l-l," letter by letter, into her palm. This intrigued Helen, even though she had no idea what this new game could entail. Other words and their corresponding objects came and went, including "m-u-g," but nothing stuck.

One day, after several weeks of much frustration, Anne held the 7-year-old Helen's one hand under the cool water of a well-pump while tracing letters into the other. Finally, Helen grasped the concept: Anne had been spelling "w-a-t-e-r." The dark veil surrounding Helen had parted, and a new world began to slowly take shape; she referred to this breakthrough as the moment her "soul was born." Helen learned a total of 30 words that day. Within six months, she'd mastered 625.

Through years of practice and study, Anne and Helen worked together to add other skills to Helen's growing repertoire, from taking notes on a typewriter to reading Shakespeare to learning foreign languages and even geometry. In 1904, Helen fulfilled her childhood dream of attending Harvard University by receiving her Bachelor of Arts degree from Radcliffe College (its women-only institution of the day), becoming the first deaf-blind person to graduate from college.

Having never forgotten the exhilaration that came from learning to engage with the world around her, Helen dedicated the rest of her life to advocating for and promoting the rights of visually impaired and deaf-blind people across the globe. And while her accolades are far too numerous to list, she was nominated for a Nobel Peace Prize in 1953 and received the Presidential Medal of Freedom from President Lyndon B. Johnson. All of which would not have been possible without the determination of her teacher. No one better than Helen can describe the selfless sentiment that fueled her life's work: "I would rather walk with a friend in the dark, than alone in the light."

Helen Keller and Anne Sullivan in an undated photo. Adapted from a 1959 play of the same title, the 1962 biographical film *The Miracle Worker* details Sullivan's work tutoring Keller.

★ AMELIA EARHART ★

HEN MANY WOMEN her age were rushing off to start a family, Amelia Earhart only had eyes for flying. After a flight with a World War I flying ace, Earhart felt compelled to take flying lessons. She chopped off her hair, started wearing a leather jacket and even bought a plane. After receiving her U.S. pilot's license, on a whim, the rookie flyer managed to coax her aircraft to a staggering 14,000 feet, setting a new record for female pilots everywhere. A short six months later, Earhart became the 16th woman to receive an international pilot's license.

Just as her new passion began to take off, Earhart faced a series of debilitating setbacks: Her inheritance completely dried up, forcing the aviatrix to sell her plane and take a job as a social worker to make ends meet, while painful sinus problems (and unsuccessful operations) kept her thoroughly grounded. Nevertheless, her refusal to give up her dream paid off. After news of Charles Lindbergh's solo flight across the Atlantic Ocean took the world by storm, Earhart received a call asking if she'd like to do the same. Within weeks, the 30-year-old made history by touching down on the other side of the pond in Wales. Over the course of 20 grueling hours, the daring aviator became the first woman to complete a transatlantic flight.

Earhart took it upon herself to keep pushing the envelope by shattering a slew

of records and undertaking harrowing solo flights from Honolulu to Oakland, California, Los Angeles to Mexico City and more. In the rare moments when she wasn't strapped into a cockpit, Earhart married her public relations manager and even lent her name to a line of women's activewear. Committed to paying it forward, she eagerly promoted The Ninety-Nines, an organization dedicated to advancing the cause of women pilots from all corners of the globe. In 1937, at the height of her fame, Earhart and navigator Fred Noonan disappeared while attempting her most ambitious feat yet: flying around the world. Though Earhart tragically never made it to her final destination, her soaring ambition still continues to inspire.

★ JAMES SMITH ★

NEARLY A DECADE before Washington crossed the Delaware, James Smith fought like hell to resist the British forces jeopardizing his community's safety. Following the French and Indian War, the Redcoats resumed trading valuable supplies with Native American tribes, a tactic that had largely helped keep the peace. As skirmishes between Native Americans and settlers grew increasingly violent, however, the colonists soon suspected their occupiers had a hand in arming the people who had massacred their villages. Smith, who himself had been attacked and taken captive by a tribe, opted to take justice into his own hands. In true "shoot first, ask questions later" fashion, the furious farmer led a group of volunteers—all dressed like Native Americans—in raiding the contents of supply wagons headed for the British-controlled Fort Pitt, determined to prove the British were conducting illegal trades of firearms and ammunition with local tribes. Obscuring their faces with paint, Smith and his comrades took things a step further by confronting another British stronghold, Fort Loudon, capturing Redcoat soldiers and releasing them in exchange for imprisoned colonists. After several months of armed resistance, the "Black Boys Rebellion" succeeded in wearing down the British, who finally abandoned the fort. Smith's message was as clear then as it is today: Americans will stand and fight to protect their own. John Wayne embodied the spirit of James Smith's valiant struggle in the film *Allegheny Uprising*.

John Wayne (as "Jim Smith") and the cast of *Allegheny Uprising* (1939).

★ SUSAN B. ANTHONY ★

FOR MANY WOMEN, owning property, casting a ballot during election season, having custody over their children and attending college aren't much to get excited about. But in the mid-19th century, each of these rights was a twinkle in Susan B. Anthony's eye.

Born and raised in a family of Quakers, Anthony grew up surrounded by abolitionists who loudly championed the radical belief that, if everyone was equal under God, that meant slaves, too. This fundamental appreciation for human rights formed a rigid moral compass, and through her involvement in abolitionist circles, Anthony came to know Frederick Douglass and Elizabeth Cady Stanton, the latter of whom became Anthony's sister-in-arms and a lifelong friend. Stanton knew just how terribly the law favored men over women, notably married women, and after recognizing in Anthony a shared hunger for righteousness, she quickly recruited her to the suffragette cause.

As part of her Quaker upbringing, Anthony also grew up involved in the temperance movement, which not only believed that drinking was sinful but a threat to public safety. At a Sons of Temperance convention in 1853, Anthony attempted to address the crowd, but was stopped. No woman would be allowed to speak. Shocked, Anthony's humiliation soon hardened into an immovable resolve: If she had to assert her rights as a woman in order to be taken seriously and further her cause, that's where she'd start.

With no husband or children in sight, Anthony devoted all of her energy and willpower to making the emancipation of women a reality. For decades, she crisscrossed the country, delivering nearly 100 lectures a year, addressing groups in bars, railroad depots, churches and, in one case, a lumber wagon. Even when confronted with dirty lodgings, disgusting food and inhospitable crowds, Anthony never lost sight of her goal. Every mile, she knew, had to be a step in the right direction. By 1869, Anthony and Stanton founded the National Woman Suffrage Association to mobilize women's rights activists across America. But as the movement grew, Anthony decided to try an unprecedented direct approach to enacting change.

On election day in 1872, Anthony showed up to the polls and cast her ballot, an act which landed her straight in jail. Her highly publicized trial began the following June, and by the second day, Justice Ward Hunt ordered the all-male jury to find Anthony guilty. But the following day, Hunt asked Anthony if she had anything to say. Seizing her one and only chance to speak, the suffragette launched into a passionate rebuke of Hunt's handling of her trial. The male jurors were her political superiors; where were her true peers? As for paying the $100 fine, she told him, "I shall never pay a dollar of your unjust penalty." Following the trial, Anthony and Stanton knew beyond a shadow of a doubt that the way forward would have to involve lobbying Congress to pass an amendment to the Constitution.

Although she didn't live to see the passing of the 19th Amendment, women today leave their "I Voted" stickers on Anthony's grave as tokens of thanks to the Quaker suffragette who demanded their rights.

★ ELEANOR ★ ROOSEVELT

 EFORE 1933, FIRST LADIES were expected to be little more than hostesses. But when Eleanor Roosevelt walked into the White House, she broke the mold.

Like many privileged girls at the turn of the century, young Eleanor was groomed to become a high society wife. Sent to finishing school abroad, she made her social debut in 1902 and soon met her future husband, Franklin Delano Roosevelt. Three years later, the couple married, and by 32, Eleanor had given birth to six children. Every inch the dutiful spouse, motherhood still left her feeling unfulfilled. Instead, she envied her husband's foray into politics as a member of the New York Senate.

In 1918, Eleanor's life turned upside down when she discovered love letters in her husband's suitcase: not only were Franklin and her secretary, Lucy Mercer, having an affair, he wanted out of their marriage. After Sara Delano Roosevelt stood by her daughter-in-law's side, threatening to disinherit her son if he followed through with his plan, Eleanor realized she had more power than she thought. Romance now cast firmly aside, she confronted Franklin about restructuring their marriage into a political partnership, and he agreed. She supported his 1920 campaign for Vice President, and despite his loss, Franklin saw his wife as an asset to his cause.

When Franklin was 39 years old, he contracted polio disease. But rather than allow him to step down from leadership, Eleanor insisted he stick to his dreams. She concealed his condition by speaking in public on his behalf and began making a name for herself on the campaign trail. With feisty Eleanor at his side, Franklin was elected Governor of New York and in 1932, the Roosevelts took the White House.

On becoming First Lady, Eleanor felt a pang of regret: Her talented, charming predecessors had all given up their passions to support their husbands; surely she would be expected to do the same. Unwilling to

Eleanor Roosevelt at the opening of the United Nations Commission on Human Rights. The trailblazing first lady broke barriers for female journalists by hosting several ladies-only press conferences at the White House.

THE UNIVERSAL DECLARATION OF **Human Rights**

conform to anyone's expectations, Eleanor hosted press conferences. She began writing a newspaper column in which she dared to share her views on politics and insights into her personal life. And for good measure, she started her own radio show. As her husband's New Deal policies helped get everyday Americans back on their feet, America was dragged into World War II. But rather than simply stay home, Eleanor flew out to visit the troops. After Franklin passed away in 1945, she was appointed a delegate to the United Nations and had a hand in drafting the Declaration of Human Rights.

By the 1950s, an elderly Eleanor opted to take her civil rights activism on a road trip throughout the south. As a former First Lady and outspoken crusader, she'd make for an easy target. But in a move that John Wayne would approve of, she carried her own protection, complete with a firearms license to prove it.

From the highest office in the land, Eleanor Roosevelt showed the world how a First Lady could do more than smile in the background—she could have a career, too.

★ INGENUITY ★

BEYOND KEEPING YOUR COMPOSURE, SOMETIMES YOU HAVE TO CALL UPON QUICK WIT TO OVERCOME A TALL TASK.

John Wayne directs on the set of *The Alamo* (1960). The film won an Academy Award for Best Sound Mixing in 1961.

BUILDING FROM THE ★ GROUND UP ★

WHETHER HE WAS HONING HIS ONSCREEN PRESENCE OR BRINGING IDEAS TO LIFE AS A DIRECTOR, DUKE'S INNOVATIVE THINKING ALWAYS CARRIED HIM ABOVE AND BEYOND.

THE CHARACTERS JOHN Wayne played throughout his career frequently found themselves cornered and outnumbered, but they were rarely outsmarted. Behind the scenes, however, the legend was also constantly proving the worth of his wit as he relied on his limitless creativity to work his way through the various challenges presented by his career.

Upon earning his big break as well as the moniker "John Wayne" with *The Big Trail* in 1930, Duke knew he had a lot to live up to. He needed to become larger-than-life in order to maintain his momentum as a Western star, and he had to do so in short order.

"When I started, I knew I was no actor, and I went to work on this Wayne thing," the legend once told *The New York Times*.

"It was as deliberate a projection as you'll ever see. I figured I needed a gimmick, so I dreamed up the drawl, the squint and a way of moving meant to suggest that I wasn't looking for trouble but would just as soon throw a bottle at your head as not. I practiced in front of a mirror." Fittingly, Duke would gain much of the inspiration for the John Wayne cinematic persona by working with a man meant to act as his mirror image. On the set of the crime serial *The Shadow of the Eagle* in 1932, the up-and-coming actor would meet Yakima Canutt, who was hired to play a henchman and also serve as Duke's stunt double. Realizing the stunt actor's rugged cowboy qualities weren't just an act but rather who he was at all times, John Wayne began to take note. In a biography, the icon recalled a particularly inspiring incident in which Canutt was dealing with some rowdy wranglers and stuntmen on set: "When in trouble, he had a half-humorous glint in his eye and talked very straight and very direct to his opponent. You had a feeling that there was a steel spring waiting to be released...."

Beyond being able to talk the talk, Duke knew "John Wayne" would also need to convincingly walk the walk. With plenty of time on set together and plenty of scraps in the scripts of the B-Westerns they starred in, the actor and Canutt would work on making every fight scene feel like the real deal. The two men developed a technique, now called the "pass system," in which the actors stand at the perfect angle in front of the camera when the punches are thrown, creating the illusion of fist-to-face contact. According to Canutt, the pair often worked to improve the method well after its inception. "John and I were so competitive and eager to top whatever stunt or fight scene we'd done before that I always thought we'd have been in real danger if we weren't good friends," the stuntman said in a biography.

John Wayne (in costume as Davy Crockett) directs Frankie Avalon (seated) and Laurence Harvey on set of *The Alamo* (1960).

John Wayne's tough-talking, fist-throwing persona on the big screen would make him a legend in the decades to come, but his career would still be met with challenges when he took his talents to the other side of the camera in the 1950s. Aiming to direct the story of the Alamo in grand fashion, Duke had a difficult time getting a movie studio to foot the bill for his passion project. After spending months shopping it around, the ambitious actor/director decided to rely on his own skill and resolve. He found investors in part by putting his money where his mouth was, ponying up $1.2 million of his own money into the project, giving *The Alamo* (1960) the big budget it needed to recreate the mission exactly as it was before its defense against Santa Anna's forces. When budget concerns meant dialing back the massive size of the set, John Wayne's compromise was to get as close as possible to the real thing, which meant the entire set be built at 75 percent scale (with the exception of the chapel, which was a full-size replica).

Armed with stone, wood from broken-down buildings, limestone and handmade adobe bricks, Duke and his crew of builders broke ground on the new Alamo in February 1958. As the replica of Old San Antonio was isolated from town, they also had to build 14 miles of road and tap several deep-water wells to keep the cast and crew supplied and hydrated. During a delay in filming, John Wayne decided they could make the 400-acre set even more epic by turning a creek into a river through a system of dikes and dams. For good measure, he also commissioned a stable that could house 1,000 horses and 300 longhorns. Unlike most movie sets, Duke's brilliantly realized vision of the Alamo remained standing and open to the public for tours until 2009—a lasting reminder of just how much craftsmanship and creativity the legend was capable of when he put his mind to a task.

★ NEIL ARMSTRONG ★

AS 600 MILLION people watched Neil Armstrong set foot on the surface of the moon, they didn't just witness an historic event for the ages—the world saw the fulfillment of a lifelong love of flight. Born in 1930, Armstrong's passion for aviation began while attending the Cleveland Air Races with his father. At 6 years old, Armstrong took his first flight in a Ford Trimotor airplane. The boy was hooked; by 15, he'd learned to fly before he even acquired a driver's license.

As an adult, he entered Purdue University on a special scholarship awarded by the U.S. Navy. It came with a catch: two years of study, followed by two years of flight training, one year as an aviator in the Navy, then the two final years of undergraduate studies. The freshman aeronautical engineer took notice when the intrepid test pilot Chuck Yeager broke the sound barrier in 1947, and thought there'd be little left to achieve. But at the outbreak of the Korean War, Armstrong put his classes on hold to serve his country as a fighter pilot, escorting planes on photo reconnaissance missions in the Korean War. Over the course of five tours and 78 combat missions, he made a name for himself as one of the best pilots in the Navy.

After wrapping up his bachelor's degree at Purdue, Armstrong took a page out of Yeager's book and became a test pilot for the National Advisory Committee for Aeronautics (NACA, the predecessor to NASA), and quickly took to the skies in experimental aircraft like the North American X-15 rocket plane, which he flew at speeds exceeding 4,500 miles per hour. After hearing of a program to recruit pilots to become astronauts, Armstrong tossed his hat into the ring and was accepted. He got the chance to prove his technical prowess in space during the Gemini 8 mission, when a stuck thruster caused his spacecraft to spin wildly out of control. He acted fast, shutting off Gemini's orbital maneuvering system and manually engaging the re-entry thrusters to stabilize the craft, preventing further disaster. Years later, while testing NASA's lunar landing vehicle in preparation for his upcoming Apollo mission, Armstrong made the correct call to eject after suddenly losing control of the machine. He safely escaped the craft just seconds before it crashed and burned, a testament to his instincts as much as his intelligence.

By the time he launched into orbit with the crew of Apollo 11, Armstrong had shown himself to be not only an accomplished flyer, but a man who'd already kept his cool under pressure in outer space. As he was stationed closest to the hatch, Armstrong got the go-ahead to depart the lunar module first and become the first human being to set foot on the surface of the moon, where he uttered the famous words, "That's one small step for man, one giant leap for mankind."

Command pilot Neil Armstrong (right) and pilot David R. Scott prepare to board the Gemini 8 module on March 16, 1966. Armstrong and Scott were forced to abort the mission due to technical difficulties, but managed to return to Earth safely on March 17.

GEORGE WASHINGTON ★ CARVER ★

THOUGH HE WASN'T responsible for the invention of peanut butter, George Washington Carver forged an even greater legacy by calling attention to the versatility of the humble peanut crop.

By 1916, the state of Alabama faced an agricultural crisis when an intrusive pest called the boll weevil destroyed its prized cotton crop. A professor at the Tuskegee Institute, Carver knew the South's overreliance on cotton had stripped its soil of nutrients. Having studied the properties of peanuts, he felt confident the cheap plant could prove a viable long-term solution and prevent further environmental catastrophe.

Carver spread his message to black sharecroppers in the form of educational horse-drawn wagons—schools-on-wheels—that took his discoveries from the lab to the field. As a proponent of sustainable farming, he argued that peanuts released nitrogen, a nutrient which could breathe life back into tired, depleted soil. Although struggling farmers were delighted to see how quickly peanuts rejuvenated their soil, they were soon dismayed at the surplus of peanuts rotting away in their stores.

Determined to help the public get the most out of their crop and break their dependence on cotton, the professor published a study in which he outlined how peanuts could be used to make more than 300 products, including shampoo, insulation, shaving cream, mayonnaise, coffee, paints and more. Armed with this new knowledge, farmers mitigated their waste and reaped serious profits, helping the South get back on its feet.

★ LEWIS & CLARK ★

FOLLOWING THE PURCHASE of the Louisiana Territory in 1803, President Thomas Jefferson enlisted his secretary, Captain Meriwether Lewis, and Lewis's good friend, William Clark, to lead an expedition of Army men to chart a passage to the Pacific Ocean. Jefferson had several goals in mind: to find a body of water suitable for conducting trade; to explore any unclaimed territory before Britain or other European countries could beat them to the punch; and to document the flora and fauna scattered along the way.

With help from a 16-year-old Shoshone interpreter, Sacagawea (who brought her infant son in a sling across her back), and Clark's slave, York, the Corps of Discovery Expedition set off from Missouri on a two-year, 8,000-mile journey to the westernmost edge of the continental U.S. Along the way, the group encountered harsh weather, frostbite, dehydration, starvation, a slew of diseases, only one death (likely from appendicitis) and dozens of Native American tribes, including the Sioux, the Chinook, the Crow and the Shoshone, where Sacagawea briefly reunited with her family. Passing through Montana and Oregon, the crew spotted the Pacific in November 1805 and set up a fort to hold out through the harsh winter. As soon as the snow melted, the expedition began its long trek home and all received a hero's welcome on their return to Missouri in 1806. Although they had failed to find the fabled Northwest Passage, through identifying 178 previously unknown plants and 122 animals, as well as forging ties with Native American tribes, Lewis and Clark's bold vision helped give Americans a clearer idea of the world that lay beyond the horizon, and ushered in an age of expansion across the American west.

★ JACK LONDON ★

ONE OF THE most celebrated writers of the 20th century, Jack London's inspiring, frontier fiction was the direct result of his own dogged determination. His biological father, William Chaney, abandoned the family shortly before London's birth in 1876. At the age of 13, London dropped out of school and began working grueling 12- to 18-hour shifts at a cannery to help support his family. Dissatisfied and miserable, he borrowed money from a family friend to buy a sloop and began poaching oysters off the California coast. But by 18, London had started running with a crowd of hobos and ne'er-do-wells. Riding the rails as far as Niagara Falls, he was arrested for vagrancy and spent a month in jail. Having reached rock bottom, the teenager took this wake-up call to heart, and when he returned home, London taught himself the classics, cramming four years' worth of foundational education into a 12-month span so he could apply to U.C. Berkeley.

Drawn to a life of adventure and short on funds to finish his education, London moved to Alaska during the Klondike Gold Rush, where he toiled as a prospector in the frigid wilderness until scurvy forced him back to California. He soon set himself on climbing out of poverty for good by honing his writing skills, drawing on his experiences to flesh out beloved novels such as *The Call of the Wild* and *White Fang*.

★ GARRETT MORGAN ★

BORN IN 1877 as the son of freed slaves, Garrett Morgan made his fortune by creating ingenious solutions to observable problems. Like many Americans around the turn of the century, Morgan was forced to drop out of school at a young age in order to support his family. Working as a handyman and, later, a repairman at a sewing machine factory, Morgan enjoyed finding new ways to make machines more efficient; in a few years, he managed to save enough money to open his own repair business.

While creating a liquid solution to keep overheated sewing needles from scorching wool fabric, Morgan accidentally discovered the same substance could be safely used to straighten hair. He named it "G.A. Morgan's Hair Refiner" and began selling it around the country with other hair products.

But just as Morgan began to make a name for himself in the garment and beauty industries, inspiration struck yet again after he witnessed a team of firemen struggling to save lives while inhaling smoke. In September 1912, he filed a patent for a smoke-proof hood device, complete with an air tube that trailed along the floor to provide the wearer with a supply of fresh air. Four years later, Morgan put his gear to the test when he rescued men trapped in a gas-filled tunnel under Lake Erie. And in 1923, in an effort to cut down on the number of car accidents he saw on the road, the inventor sold the patent for his three-way traffic light signal to General Electric Company for $40,000.

Lucille Ball gets close with John Wayne in 1955. That year, Duke appeared as himself in an episode of *I Love Lucy* titled "Lucy and John Wayne."

★ LUCILLE BALL ★

BORN AUGUST 6, 1911, in Jamestown, New York, to Henry and Désirée (DeDe), Lucille Ball's earliest memories were of tragedy and instability. When she was only 3 years old, her father died of typhoid fever. Soon after, her mother remarried and moved to Detroit, leaving Ball behind in Jamestown with her stepfather's mother, a woman whose strict beliefs wouldn't allow mirrors in the house for fear they might encourage vanity. But on the rare occasions she snuck a peek at her reflection, Ball took the opportunity to explore her expressive face—a skill she would later use to make her mark on the world.

By the time she was reunited with her mother, Ball was restlessly entering her teenage years with dreams of show business. At 15, she enrolled in the John Murray Anderson School for the Dramatic Arts in New York City, where she initially struggled to the point that her teachers wrote to her mother, "Lucy's wasting her time and ours." Despite the feedback, Ball stayed in school to hone her craft. By 1927, she was doing chorus work on Broadway; and in the early 1930s, she headed to Hollywood. Much like her eventual friend John Wayne, Ball took any and all film work she could find, earning herself the nickname "Queen of the Bs." Aside from her B-movie career, Ball also did radio work and continued to perform on Broadway.

During this time, she met bandleader Desi Arnaz on the set of the musical *Too Many Girls*, eloping less than six months after they first met. With almost 20 years of hard work under her belt, Ball's life would change in 1948 when she was cast in the radio program *My Favorite Husband*. Recognizing her gifts for physical comedy, she would adapt the program to television under the title *I Love Lucy*.

Thanks to Ball's incomparable comedic timing and unique relatability, *I Love Lucy* became a family viewing ritual all across America. The show's humor cleverly disguised its progressive undertones, bringing issues such as gender inequality to light while remaining enjoyable for all audiences. Using her position at Desilu, the production company she founded with Arnaz, Ball radically changed the television industry; *I Love Lucy* was the first show to use three cameras to shoot in front of a live audience, the first to record using film, the first to syndicate and air reruns, the first to feature an interracial couple and the first to have a pregnant actress playing a pregnant character. She even invited her friend, John Wayne, to come join the fun for his own episode. Ball's decision to blend her personal and professional lives carried her to success for decades to come. Through pursuing risky, innovative ideas, Lucille Ball forged an iconic career for herself and paved the way for countless others to do the same.

ALEXANDER ★ GRAHAM BELL ★

WHILE ALEXANDER GRAHAM Bell is most famous for patenting the telephone, his passion for deaf education remains one of his most profound endeavors. Born in Scotland to a line of speech therapists, Bell grew up with a special awareness of the nature of sound when his mother began to lose hearing during his childhood. Through trial and error, he discovered he could still convey things to his mother by getting very close to her forehead and speaking directly at it in slow, measured tones, allowing her to feel the vibrations of his voice. He also began communicating with her by using his fingers to tap out conversations taking place at their house.

After the Bell family relocated to the United States, Bell continued to study how proper enunciation and other aspects of elocution could be used to help deaf or mute people better integrate into society. Despite his lack of a formal background in the subject, he opened a school for the deaf in which he taught a transcribed phonetics system that would allow deaf people to learn to speak.

Driven by a desire to replicate and record the human voice, following hundreds of hours of experimenting, at 29, he filed his patent for the telephone. More than 500 lawsuits would soon follow, but Bell held fast to his claims and won. Among his many inventions, Bell even patented a metal detector with which he tried to locate the fatal bullet that lodged in President James Garfield. His contributions paved the way for communication as we know it today.

RALPH BUNCHE ★

AS AN AFRICAN American growing up in the early 20th century, Ralph Bunche resolved to be proud of his heritage no matter what discrimination he faced. The future "Father of Peacekeeping" excelled academically, climbing to the top of his class in high school, college and grad school, going so far as to earn his doctoral degree in political science at Harvard.

Bunche put his studies to the test in the U.S. State Department, from which he segued into the newly-formed United Nations. Shifting his focus to a global scale, he was drawn to negotiating an end to the oldest animosity in the world: the conflict between the Arabs and Israelis. When the U.N.'s lead mediator, Count Folke Bernadotte of Sweden, suggested Jerusalem be put under Arab control, he was shot to death, leaving Bunche to pick up the pieces in the wake of his colleague's tragic demise. Knowing any more missteps could cost him his life, the newly senior emissary saw his own struggle against prejudice mirrored in the struggle to bring about a peaceful discourse in the Holy Land. He arranged a rendezvous with the Israeli representative, but rather than meet in an office, the two spoke casually over a game of billiards. Bunche's personable approach ultimately won over the Israelis, who agreed to armistice negotiations with the Palestinians. For his efforts in bringing the war to an end, Bunche became the first African American to receive the Nobel Peace Prize and was later awarded the Presidential Medal of Freedom.

★ MAYA ANGELOU ★

 WHEN WE USE the term "Renaissance Man" we're usually talking about someone who, because of their high station in life, was able to forge a path in a number of disciplines at once. Likewise, when we use the term "Jack of All Trades," we're usually referring to someone who, out of curiosity, necessity or a combination of the two, learned how to excel in a number of different roles. Maya Angelou was someone who, becoming the latter at a young age, was able to work her way up to being the former. A poet, novelist, playwright, civil rights activist and the recipient of more than 50 honorary degrees, Angelou died a Renaissance Woman. The experience that led her to this exalted post, however, is not one from which our most celebrated intellectual figures come.

Born Marguerite Annie Johnson in St. Louis, Missouri, in 1928, Maya Angelou was the child of a Navy dietician and a nurse. When she was three, her parents' marriage ended and Angelou was sent to Arkansas to live with her grandmother. She was later shuffled to St. Louis, where she lived with her mother and her boyfriend, a man who unfortunately turned out to be abusive. When she testified to his crimes, he received only a day in jail but was soon murdered, presumably by Angelou's male

family members. Convinced her speaking up had gotten him killed, the frightened child refused to speak for five years, all the while developing a remarkable memory.

Adulthood for a woman of color in St. Louis in the first half of the 20th century was a low-odds proposition at the best of times, and Angelou's less-than-stable home situation led her to take jobs as a dancer, singer, musician and actress. While struggling to make ends meet, she learned to speak several foreign languages and became close with some of the founders of the modern civil rights movement. By the 1960s she was close friends with Malcolm X and her writing and performing were of such obvious quality that shortly before his assassination, Martin Luther King Jr. tapped Angelou to organize a civil rights march.

Despite not having attended college, Angelou created a literary oeuvre that appeals to academics and casual readers alike. Her gritty, realistic depictions of the hardships of everyday life are brilliantly contrasted with an uncanny ability to highlight the beauty in other, just as pedestrian, items and situations. She wasn't dealt the strongest hand, but thanks to her intelligence, drive and unwavering grace, Maya Angelou taught a generation of Americans the enduring power of empathy and willpower.

★ THOMAS EDISON ★

THE UNITED STATES of America is a country famous for its unyielding work ethic, and many of our cultural heroes betray our admiration for those willing to steamroll the competition through sheer elbow grease. Thomas Edison is one of the purest examples of this kind of hero: a blunt object of ambition and know-how whose workshop invented or patented many of the most important new products of the 20th century. His reputation for innovation formed the basis of a business empire whose infrastructure still exists today.

Born in Milan, Ohio, in 1847, Thomas Alva Edison worked as a telegraph operator as a young man and attended the prestigious Cooper Union in New York for chemistry classes. After holding a string of jobs, Edison patented his first invention. An electric mechanism for vote counting, it didn't sell but foreshadowed the importance electricity would have on his career. Soon, he caught his first big break with a telegraph able to send up to four messages simultaneously. He opened his famous Menlo Park laboratory

with the proceeds in 1876, providing the base from which his invention empire would radiate across the country.

A total of 1,093 patents would be granted to designs from Edison's workshop, an output that dwarfs all other American inventors and gives credence to Edison's famous quip that genius is 1% inspiration and 99% perspiration. The country at large first took notice of Edison's talent in 1877 when he produced the first phonograph, which played music from metal cylinders— the forerunner to the vinyl record and all the hi-fi it spawned. The following year he began his work on the incandescent light bulb that would soon light homes and businesses across the world.

Throughout his time directing a laboratory so dedicated to exploring new technologies, Edison was also constantly attempting to improve existing technologies.

A number of his patents, for example, are for items like improved microphones for early transmitters (phones) and improved delivery systems for his electric light. But it's the society-changing inventions we tend to gravitate toward when discussing Edison, and there is no shortage of them. Edison's workshop was responsible for the first fluoroscope, the first American movie camera and hundreds of components that make modern electric appliances possible.

Through the sheer output he was able to produce in his lifetime with the help of the brilliant minds assembled at his workshop, Edison helped define the modern world by giving it a second "Let there be light." His myriad inventions represent a lifetime of trial and error, but as he famously said, he never failed—he only found 10,000 ways that didn't work.

★ JOHN DEERE ★

AS AMERICANS TRAVELED west to fulfill their Manifest Destiny in the early half of the 19th century, they encountered a number of unforeseen setbacks with the changing terrain. One of those settlers was blacksmith John Deere. Born in 1804 and raised in Vermont, at 33, Deere moved to Illinois and quickly set up shop selling horseshoes, sickles and other farming essentials. The craftsman met neighbors whose wood and cast iron plows broke far more often than he'd ever seen back home in New England. Tilling the thick, clay-based soil of the Illinois prairie proved more challenging than anyone had anticipated; dirt kept sticking to the farming equipment, meaning after every few yards, farmhands would have to pause their grueling work just to clean the plow.

Deere and his business partner, Major Leonard Andrus, got to work designing a series of plow shapes, and after years of trial and error, hit upon the novel idea of using highly polished steel to create a self-scouring plow, one whose unique, curved shape eliminated the need for manual cleaning. Unlike other blacksmiths, Deere went out and toiled in the fields to demonstrate the efficacy of his tools for farmers to witness firsthand. He also had the foresight to produce more plows than he'd received orders for, and as word of mouth began to spread, more orders kept flooding in, validating his instincts. Soon, Deere made a deal with steel manufacturers in Pittsburgh to create strong, sleek farming equipment to sell across the prairies, and once his son and son-in-law joined the growing business, Deere & Company was born, paving the way for an American farming revolution.

★ ALBERT EINSTEIN ★

A T THE DAWN of the 20th century, the world's most accomplished experts in the fields of physics (and by extension, everyone else) held fast to the theories that made Sir Isaac Newton a household name—mostly, that gravity is the force which causes things to fall and the means by which everyone is held firmly to the ground. Despite Newton's refusal to explain the machinations of his theory, the scientific community largely stuck to these principles since Newton first proposed them in 1687.

Enter Albert Einstein, who published a series of groundbreaking papers which forever changed our understanding of the ways the universe works. Over the course of several months, he established how to size molecules in a liquid and ascertain their movement and how light is actually made up of tiny particles called photons (which later won him the 1921 Nobel Prize). He issued a direct challenge to Newton by declaring that gravity, rather than being an all-encompassing force, is actually a curving or distorting of space, and the more massive an object, the more it stretches physical space and dilates time itself. He laid down the most famous mathematical equation in history to illustrate the mind-blowing concept that matter and energy are, at least on an atomic level, interchangeable: $E = mc^2$. But these radical new concepts went largely unheeded until 1919, when British astronomer Arthur Eddington confirmed the truth of Einstein's genius through an experiment with a solar eclipse. The German theoretical physicist saw his name splashed across the front pages of international newspapers practically overnight.

Rather than rest on his laurels or retreat to the private confines of his study, Einstein used his newfound platform to publicly champion other causes dear to him, namely by criticizing his homeland's entry into World War I. The ardent pacifist made the stunning move to rebuke Germany's militarism, denouncing its role in instigating the conflict, winning him a number of critics and enemies; one of them, Nobel Prize-winning physicist and ardent supporter of Adolf Hitler, Johannes Stark, went so far as to smear Einstein's theory of relativity as mere "Jewish propaganda physics." With antisemitism and German nationalism on the rise, the Jewish theoretical physicist knew his days in the country as a freethinking academic were numbered. He was right again.

In early 1933, the Gestapo raided Einstein's Berlin home as well his summer cottage. His worst fears confirmed, he fled to the U.S. and settled in Princeton, New Jersey. But before long, the political refugee noticed his new home had its own racial prejudices. Never one to step down from voicing inconvenient truths, Einstein lent his support to the National Association for the Advancement of Colored People and advocated for civil rights. And as Germany prepared to wage yet another massive war, he became a U.S. citizen in 1940 and wrote to President Roosevelt, urging the U.S. to use his atomic theory to develop an atomic bomb before the Germans could do so first. It was a decision he came to regret following the bombing of Japan, but one that ended the conflict in the Pacific and kept America safe. While his theories prove no easy task to grasp, Einstein's work will continue to expand our knowledge of the universe for generations to come.

★ BUZZ ALDRIN ★

WHEN NASA WAS putting together a team of astronauts to carry out their most ambitious project yet, they deferred to the technical expertise of Buzz Aldrin. After graduating third in his class at West Point, Aldrin joined the U.S. Air Force and became a fighter pilot, flying a total of 66 combat missions in the Korean War. Later, Aldrin enrolled at the Massachusetts Institute of Technology, where he earned a doctoral degree in astronautics. His flying experience, combined with his brilliant dissertation on the piloting of spacecrafts in orbit—which featured docking techniques astronauts still employ to this day—quickly got NASA's attention, and by 1963 he'd been selected for training to become an astronaut. On his first trip into orbit, during the 1966 Gemini 12 mission with Jim Lovell, Aldrin logged a record-breaking five-hour spacewalk in which he worked outside

the spacecraft. He also got the chance to put his thesis to the test when the onboard radar failed to work, forcing him to carry out all of the docking maneuvers himself.

Aldrin's finest hour came as his lunar module prepared to land on the surface of the moon on July 20, 1969. Hours after touching down in the Sea of Tranquility, Aldrin and Neil Armstrong became the first two human beings to set foot on the moon. "Beautiful view." he remarked. "Magnificent desolation." All three men of the Apollo 11 crew received the Presidential Medal of Freedom from President Richard Nixon for their fulfillment of President John F. Kennedy's call to land on the moon.

★ MOE BERG ★

MORRIS BERG was born in Harlem, New York, in 1902, a few years after the U.S. had finished its war with Spain. During that time, a conflict on the scale of World War I was unthinkable, let alone a global threat like organized fascism. But as he worked his way from the city to Princeton and later Columbia Law, and by the time the names Hitler and Tojo appeared in newspapers, Berg was a wily veteran in the rough-and-tumble field of professional baseball. Despite his enviable Ivy League education, Berg sought to prove his prowess in the outfield.

Baseball was hardly his only racket, however: as a contestant on the radio game show *Information, Please*, Berg became a minor celebrity, and thanks to his ability to speak multiple languages and retain information at an astonishing rate, the U.S. government took notice. They hired the ballplayer to work as a spy while on the road, his role on the team allowing him to hide in plain sight. The biggest mission of his career came when the U.S. sent an All-Star baseball team including Lou Gehrig and Babe Ruth to Japan in 1934. While the rest of the team played ball, Berg traveled to a hospital under the premise of visiting an American ambassador's daughter. But when he arrived, he traveled straight up to the roof, where he

used a film camera to record rare footage of Tokyo and its harbor. Later, he accepted a job with the Secret Intelligence branch of the Office of Strategic Services, touring Europe to meet with physicists and persuade them to come to the U.S. For his years of service, President Harry Truman awarded Berg the Medal of Freedom.

★ ELLA FITZGERALD ★

AS A TEENAGER growing up during the Great Depression, Ella Fitzgerald experienced more than her fair share of the blues. The future 13-time Grammy-winning "First Lady of Song" was close with her mother and enjoyed listening to jazz albums by Bing Crosby, Louis Armstrong and the Boswell Sisters. But when Fitzgerald's mother died following a car accident, the teenager found herself alone with an abusive stepfather before becoming a ward of the state, sent to live at a reform school where staff regularly beat her. Stuck in a downward spiral, she skipped classes and took work wherever she could find it, whether that meant dancing on the streets of Harlem or serving as a lookout for a local brothel.

When the Apollo Theater began hosting an amateur night, Fitzgerald signed up on a dare. On the night of her performance, however, the 17-year-old realized to her horror she'd been scheduled to follow the Edwards Sisters, a well-loved dancing duo who electrified local audiences with their fancy footwork and costumes. Knowing she wouldn't hold a candle to their polished prowess, Fitzgerald made the last-minute decision to sing "Judy,"

a song she knew by heart from listening to her idol, Connee Boswell. Floored by the richness and purity of her voice, the crowd demanded she sing another number, and by the end of the night, she took home first prize, a humble start to a stunning career as one of America's most innovative voices.

COL. HARLAND ★ SANDERS ★

BEFORE HE BUILT a finger-lickin' fast food empire on a unique blend of 11 herbs and spices, Colonel Harland Sanders of Kentucky Fried Chicken fame spent his childhood cooking and caring for his siblings while their mother toiled for days on end at a tomato cannery. After dropping out of school at 12, Sanders took work where he could get it as a farmhand, streetcar conductor, life insurance salesman and lawyer until one courtroom dispute with a client ended in an all-out brawl. But it wasn't until 1930, when he acquired a highway service station in Corbin, Kentucky, that the Colonel finally got a taste of his true calling.

At his humble roadside restaurant, Sanders served up the country-style eats he'd dished out for his family like country ham, hot biscuits, steaks and fried chicken. His café proved popular, and by 1935, Sanders was welcomed as an honorary Kentucky Colonel. As business took off and hungry travelers filled tables, the Colonel knew he needed a way to speed up the 35 minutes it took to pan fry chicken. Rather than resort to deep frying, Sanders customized a pressure cooker to work like a pressure fryer, cutting down on cooking time without sacrificing flavor. And when he learned a new interstate would divert business from his restaurant, the 65-year-old closed up shop and took his Southern hospitality on the road, selling his secret blend to restaurants across the country to start a nationwide franchise.

★ TEMPLE GRANDIN ★

MOST COWBOY MOVIES don't focus on cows. Hollywood executives during the genre's golden age felt audiences would take far greater interest in saloon fights and shootouts than the more mundane challenges of raising and maintaining a herd of cattle. For the most part, directors felt content including cows as, at best, a prop, and more often, as grass-chewing background actors.

Given the state of the cattle industry in the 1970s, any movie examining the real-life challenges of raising the animals would more closely resemble a horror film than a sweeping Western epic. "There was a tremendous amount of rough, cruel handling of cattle," Dr. Temple Grandin, a world-renowned expert in animal science and livestock management, once explained to *John Wayne Magazine*. Grandin, who started working at feedyards in 1970s Arizona, said she routinely witnessed workers shocking cattle with electrified prods repeatedly, killing animals by jacking up the hydraulic pressure in cattle chutes and, in one instance, breaking a calf's neck while wrestling with it. "That was a bad era where some workers didn't see the cattle as living creatures with feeling," said Grandin. But for Grandin, who credits her unique visual imagination with allowing her to see the world through an animal's eyes, took an ingenious new approach, one that revolutionized the relationship between the herder and the herd.

Grandin started that revolution with her design of a dip vat at an Arizona feedyard in '76. Before Grandin, ranch hands forced the terrified cattle to walk, jam-packed, down a concrete slope to submerge themselves in a seven-foot-deep pool of insecticide and then emerge on the other side. It was dangerous, and often deadly, for the cattle. Grandin designed a more gradual concrete decline with grooves over its surface, which made the process safer for the animals.

Grandin's ideas found slow acceptance among the hardened cowboys who had been raising cattle for generations, but she was determined to change their minds. "I think a lot of the pushback was because I was a girl going into a man's industry," Grandin said. One place more accepting was John Wayne's Red River Feedyard, which she joined in '78. "It was a dream job," she said.

The success Grandin found at John Wayne's Red River Feedyard and other ranches in Arizona gave her then-unorthodox techniques the boost of credibility needed to help transform the way cowboys look at cattle. Today, Grandin's principles of designing livestock facilities to provide cattle with a low-stress environment have become the new standard. "There's a lot of interest in not yelling at the cattle while handling them, moving them in small groups and being quiet while working with them," said Grandin. "When I first started talking about those things, in the '70s and '80s, I was laughed at. Now, people take it seriously."

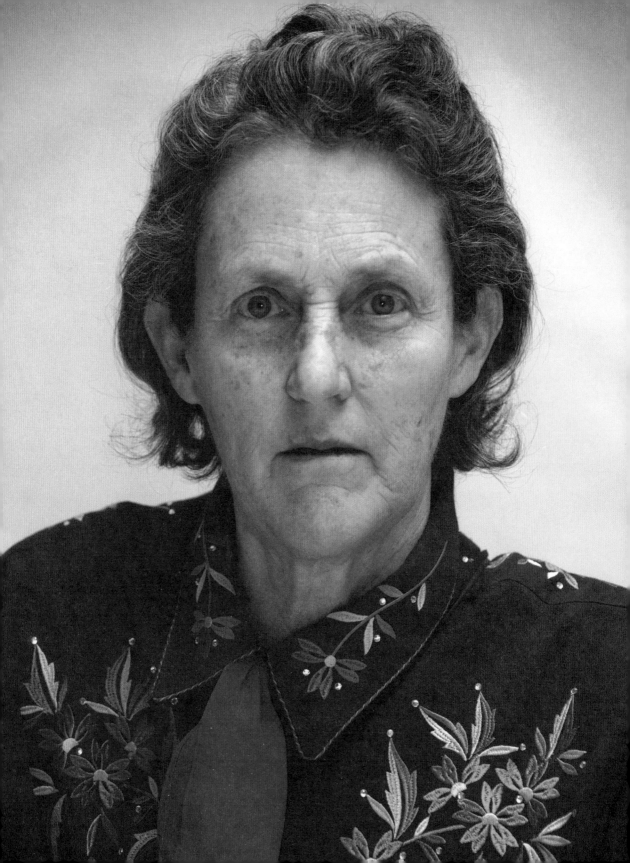

★ JONAS SALK ★

AMERICANS TODAY can thank Jonas Salk for not having to experience the disabling disease of paralytic poliomyelitis, commonly known as polio. Born in 1914, as the child of working-class Russian Jewish immigrants, Salk possessed neither the financial means nor the social standing necessary to gain entry into the most prestigious New York educational establishments. But he quickly developed a strong work ethic while attending public school, and by 20, Salk had enrolled at New York University to study medicine.

Salk got his first taste of the rest of his life's work in virology while working in a laboratory under the supervision of seasoned bacteriologist Dr. Thomas Francis, Jr. As he familiarized himself with the properties of the recently discovered influenza virus, Salk began to question the conventional wisdom of using live viruses in immunizations. Rather than risk infecting patients with live strains of polio, he wondered, if the diphtheria and tetanus vaccines (which featured inactive microbial toxins) had proven effective cures, why not devise a similar cure for polio? With Francis's guidance, Salk conducted an experiment in which he injected mice with a strain of influenza he had "killed" under ultraviolet light. His hypothesis was correct: the mice produced the desired antibodies without contracting the flu.

Throwing himself into his studies, Salk earned his M.D., completed his residency at Mount Sinai Hospital and received a research fellowship at the University of Michigan to develop an influenza vaccine, where he reunited with Francis and learned the proper methodology behind creating safe and effective vaccines. By 1947, the virologist received his most important role yet when he was assigned to lead the Virus Research Laboratory at the University of Pittsburgh School of Medicine. Armed with funding from the National Foundation for Infantile Paralysis (later known as the March of Dimes Foundation), Salk could get to work applying his "killed virus" technique to develop a polio vaccine.

After isolating a suitably inactive strain of polio, confident in the safety of his work, Salk put his skills to the ultimate test by injecting himself, his wife and their three sons with the vaccine, putting everyone at risk of varying degrees of paralysis and even death. His calculated gamble paid off exactly as it had with the lab mice: everyone produced antibodies without contracting the disease or experiencing any other negative symptoms.

As word of his project spread, Salk gained more funding, allowing him to administer his vaccine to more than one million children. On April 12, 1955, Francis addressed a crowd of reporters at the University of Michigan to declare the results of his former pupil's field study were in: Salk's polio vaccine was officially "safe, effective and potent." Motivated only by a desire to help humanity, Salk chose not to patent his vaccine so that future generations could live without fear of paralysis. He was later awarded the Presidential Medal of Freedom.

★ JIM ABBOTT ★

ORN WITHOUT A right hand, Jim Abbott committed himself to playing baseball at 5 years old. Long before he hit the big leagues, the tough-as-nails lefty mastered his hand-eye coordination skills by bouncing a rubber ball off of a wall for hours, perfecting his throwing and catching abilities. With his father's help, Abbott devised an ingenious way to fluidly transfer his glove to his hand immediately after hurling a pitch, allowing him to quickly field and throw with the same arm. When he had the chance to use a mechanical hand prosthesis, Abbott opted to go without. Year after year, season after season, Abbott silenced the skeptics by pitching his heart out on the field.

The Toronto Blue Jays made an offer to draft Abbott right out of high school, but rather than go pro right away, the promising pitcher elected to go to college. As a student at the University of Michigan, Abbott joined the U.S. baseball team in the 1988 Summer Olympics and pitched the final game, sealing their win against Japan. That same year, he signed a contract with the California Angels. Abbott later played with the New York Yankees, where he logged a no-hitter during the '93 season, a feat accomplished only 303 other times. Despite his disability, he managed to do with one hand what some gifted athletes could barely achieve with two, throwing fastballs that topped out at an enviable 95 miles per hour.

MADAM C.J. ★ WALKER ★

ORPHANED AT 7, married at 14 and widowed at 20, Madam C.J. Walker summoned all of her willpower to rise above her circumstances and become the first black female millionaire. As an African American woman in the latter half of the 19th century, Walker suffered from hair and scalp problems like severe dandruff and bald patches,

owing in part to the harsh chemicals commonly found in soaps of that time. After seeking advice from her older brothers who'd found work as barbers in St. Louis, Walker learned the ins-and-outs of proper hair and skin hygiene. She soon landed a job for a local businesswoman selling hair products for African American women door-to-door, offering complimentary demonstrations for interested potential customers. Before long, Walker developed her own special formula, and in 1910, the intrepid hairdresser founded the Madam C.J. Walker Manufacturing Company in Indianapolis.

As demand for her hair creams and pomades increased, Walker trained women to sell her line of products for her and started advertising her goods in newspapers across the country. She built a factory to mass produce her wares, created a beauty school and expanded her line of ointments internationally, catering to clients in the Caribbean and Central America. But even while she amassed a fortune revolutionizing the haircare industry for African American consumers, the self-made entrepreneur made sure to give back to her community, pledging funds to the Tuskegee Institute, serving on the New York chapter of the NAACP and more.

BENJAMIN ★ FRANKLIN ★

 BETTER THAN PERHAPS any individual member of his legendary generation, Benjamin Franklin represents the colonial American ideal of a man who made his own way in the world and became a leader through self-education and an adventurous spirit. Born in Boston in 1706, Franklin stopped attending school at 10 and apprenticed for his older brother, a printer. As Franklin learned this trade he also began to understand its importance for the spread of information and by 15 he was satirically taking his fellow New Englanders to task in the "Silence Dogood" letters, an early example of Franklin's dedication to free speech.

At 17, he ran away from Boston and began a new life in Philadelphia, the city with which he is most closely associated to this day. Working in print shops across the city eventually earned him a trip to London, where he continued his trade and brought back the know-how necessary to start his own newspaper, which he did in 1729. By 1733 he had become a best-selling author with *Poor Richard's Almanac*. He had reached the pinnacle of his chosen trade, and was ready for new ones.

With the financial success that his career as a writer was bringing him, Franklin was able to embark on a number of new endeavors. He began experimenting with electricity and invented the lightning rod. He invented both bifocal eyeglasses and the "Franklin Stove," a metal-encased fireplace-shaped appliance. He was instrumental in the founding of both the University of Pennsylvania and the first fire department in the city of Philadelphia. Yet, as far as his stamp on American history was concerned, he'd only just begun.

Having been an outspoken advocate for free speech since his teenage years, Franklin was immediately drawn to talk of the 13 British North American Colonies gaining their independence. He had in fact been one of America's most persuasive and eloquent statesmen going back to the French and Indian War, but as the revolution approached, Franklin became the elder statesman of the newly declared colonies, making his way around the world to convince foreign governments that the American experiment was a worthwhile one. As the U.S.'s first envoy to France and first Postmaster General, Franklin helped usher the new nation into world affairs more than any of his more militarily inclined contemporaries could have, proving Americans were more than just upstart provincials. He showed the world that like him, we were formidable, savvy and multi-talented.

THURGOOD ★ MARSHALL ★

BORN IN 1908 as the son of a railroad porter, Thurgood Marshall developed a love for debate early in life, accompanying his father to watch court cases in Baltimore, Maryland, and discussing the various proceedings on their way home. An eager student with an eye for detail, when Marshall decided he wanted to pursue law as his calling, his mother offered up a precious downpayment—pawning her engagement and wedding rings so that her son could enroll at Howard University Law School. To pay her back, he graduated first in his class in 1933 and went on to head the Legal Defense Fund for the National Association for the Advancement of Colored People.

Marshall made it his life's mission to overturn "separate but equal" policies against African Americans that had been made legal under *Plessy v. Ferguson* (1896). In 1946, the lawyer put his life on the line following a court case in Columbia, Tennessee, in which he was arrested on trumped-up charges, thrown into a sheriff's car and driven off a main road. Fortunately, his colleagues never gave up the chase, and eventually Marshall was released.

Despite these threats, Marshall soldiered on, and in 1954, he successfully argued before the U.S. Supreme Court that racial segregation in public schools was unconstitutional in the landmark case *Brown v. Board of Education of Topeka.* President John F. Kennedy took notice of his civil rights successes, eventually appointing Marshall to the U.S. Court of Appeals for the Second Circuit, and with President Lyndon B. Johnson's nomination, Marshall became the first African American justice to serve on the Supreme Court.

THE CREW OF
★ APOLLO 13 ★

ON APRIL 11, 1970, Apollo 13 took off from Kennedy Space Center on a voyage to the surface of the moon. Fifty-five hours into the mission, minutes after wrapping up a live television broadcast, the three astronauts—Jim Lovell, Jack Swigert and Fred Haise—felt a "short bang and vibration." Warning lights flashed: an oxygen tank on their service module (SM) had just exploded, causing another tank to fail as well. Since the oxygen supply was connected to the fuel cells that powered the spacecraft, this meant a devastating loss in power as well. Lovell looked out a window to see precious oxygen venting into space, while Swigert broke the news to mission control: "Houston, we've had a problem here."

With 15 minutes of electricity left in the SM, the astronauts knew the main objective could no longer involve landing on the moon, but making it home alive. Their mission aborted, Houston told the crew to power down the command module (CM) before moving into the lunar module (LM), which had enough water, power and oxygen to sustain two men over the course of two days. Now the team would need to stretch those numbers to support three men for four days.

To change their trajectory from a path that would land on the moon to one that would send them around it, the crew briefly engaged the LM descent propulsion system, counting on the moon's gravitational pull to essentially slingshot their spacecraft on a looped return back to Earth.

But before long, the astronauts became aware of the rising carbon dioxide levels. On the ground, experts at mission control raced to find a way to adapt the square-shaped filtration system from the CM to fit the round-shaped openings of the LM, using only materials found in the spacecraft and relaying their findings to the astronauts.

The crew powered down the LM to conserve the rest of their limited resources, drinking six ounces of water a day and subsisting largely off what little food did not require rehydration to eat. Over the next few days, the men lost a combined 31 pounds, while the temperature inside the spacecraft fell as low as 38 degrees. Finally, the team got the go-ahead to power up and enter the CM for the final leg of the trip home. They disconnected from the LM and the SM before re-entering earth's atmosphere, plunging down in the Pacific Ocean on April 17, 1970. For their bravery and quick thinking when impossible odds were stacked against them, each crewmember received a Presidential Medal of Freedom.

ALEXANDER ★ HAMILTON ★

BORN IN THE Caribbean to unwed parents, Alexander Hamilton learned to lean on his intellect as a way to advance his social standing early in life. His father abandoned the family, his mother died of yellow fever and before he'd turned 18, a major hurricane destroyed much of the island he called home. Putting pen to paper, Hamilton recorded his own thoughts about the tempest, and his eloquent, spirited prose soon caught the attention of charitable minds in the American colonies. Within months of the storm, Hamilton was spirited away to New York City to pursue a formal education.

Talk of revolution in the colonies soon turned from a whisper to a roar, and Hamilton volunteered to take up the fight against British tyranny; he served as General George Washington's aide-de-camp before leading a battalion in attacking British forces at Yorktown, a decisive victory that helped the Continental Army win the war. Once back in New York, Hamilton threw himself into his studies, determined to become a lawyer.

As the newly-freed colonies grappled with creating a democratized system of government, the nation's brightest minds converged to form the Articles of Confederation, and later the Constitution. Hamilton took it upon himself to join forces with John Jay and James Madison to write dozens of anonymous articles generating support for the ratification of the Constitution; out of the 85 articles in The Federalist Papers, he reportedly contributed a staggering 51. In 1789, President Washington appointed his former aide to be the first Secretary of the United States Treasury. In this role, Hamilton aimed to pay back the nation's war debts in full. He established the fledgling country's financial system, created the first national bank and the United States Mint. He even managed to win over the support of more-power-to-the-states, diehard Democratic-Republican Thomas Jefferson with a calculated compromise, agreeing to move the nation's capital from New York City to Washington, D.C.

However, after President Washington unexpectedly stepped down and made room for John Adams to take his place as commander-in-chief, with his mentor no longer in the picture, Hamilton quickly discovered he'd made quite a few enemies, including Adams, Jefferson, Madison and Aaron Burr, a fellow lawyer and war veteran whom Hamilton had gradually come to know and dislike.

Hamilton did not believe John Adams or Thomas Jefferson had the vision or drive to see through the duties of the office as president in the way that Washington had intended and made no secret of his discontent. By the election of 1800, he started publishing his personal detractions of Adams's character, hoping to sway the outcome. But when it became clear that Burr and Jefferson were tied, Hamilton chose what he viewed to be the lesser evil and backed Jefferson, a sleight that Burr could not ignore. Burr challenged Hamilton to a duel on July 11, 1804. And while Hamilton threw away his shot, Burr's bullet hit its mark, and Hamilton died of his wounds the following day.

BOOKER T. ★ WASHINGTON ★

B ORN INTO SLAVERY in 1856, Booker T. Washington spent the first few years of his life on a tobacco farm hauling sacks of grain to be ground at a mill. But even after President Abraham Lincoln freed the slaves with the passing of the Emancipation Proclamation, life in the Reconstruction Era proved challenging for African Americans, and an education was a luxury few could afford. At 9 years old, Washington was put to work in a salt furnace with his stepfather. Sympathetic to her son's desire to learn, Washington's mother gave him a book. Every morning, he would wake up well before dawn to teach himself how to read and write before heading off to work.

After the end of the Civil War, Washington left home in 1872, walking 500 miles to the Hampton Normal Agricultural Institute in Virginia, where he lobbied for a chance to study in exchange for working on the grounds as a janitor. His impeccable work ethic left an impression on the school's founder, General Samuel C. Armstrong, who offered the enterprising young man a scholarship. Washington completed his studies three years later, earning top marks, at which point Gen. Armstrong offered him a teaching position. In 1881, when the general was asked to recommend a white man to lead the all-black Tuskegee Normal and Industrial Institute, he ignored their stipulation and insisted he knew the perfect man for the job. At 25 years old, just 16 years after gaining his freedom, Washington became the first president of the Tuskegee Institute.

Under his careful leadership, Tuskegee grew into one of the finest academic institutions in the country, boasting a $2 million endowment. But unlike other African American leaders, Washington took a controversial stance on the "separate but equal" policies of the era. Having experienced living in slavery firsthand, he knew the Emancipation Proclamation did not put a stop to the simmering racial hatred in the South. Rather than insist black students be allowed to attend all-white schools and risk losing everything he'd built, Washington reassured the African American community that the road to equality began with pursuing an education, even if that meant attending an all-black school. While this approach earned him a few critics, it likely provided Washington's school the fighting chance it needed to survive.

In 1896, Washington became the first African American to receive an honorary masters' degree from Harvard University. Five years later, after Washington published his wildly popular second autobiography, *Up from Slavery*, President Theodore Roosevelt invited him to dine at the White House, an unprecedented move that infuriated southern statesmen. But the respect conveyed by Roosevelt's gesture spoke louder than their insults, and Washington continued to make friends in high places who were sympathetic to his cause, including Andrew Carnegie, John D. Rockefeller, J.P. Morgan and Julius Rosenwald. Through their generosity, Washington ensured institutions like Tuskegee would have the funds to continue to help the black community long after his death.

★ RESILIENCE ★

WHEN LIFE THROWS YOU TO THE GROUND, THE ONLY WAY TO KEEP MOVING FORWARD IS TO DUST YOURSELF OFF AND SADDLE UP AGAIN.

John Wayne in *The Sons of Katie Elder* (1965). Duke insisted on performing his own stunts while making the film.

BOUNCING BACK FROM ★ "THE BIG C" ★

A LIFE-THREATENING DISEASE WASN'T ENOUGH TO KEEP JOHN WAYNE OUT OF ACTION FOR LONG.

 BOTH ON SCREEN and off, John Wayne became legendary for his ability to withstand seemingly anything thrown his way. Despite the criticisms and financial failures of his earliest films, Duke kept his dreams alive thanks to his ability to put his head down while keeping his chin up as he toiled away climbing the Hollywood ladder. As a result, he went on to portray countless iconic characters who similarly proved their grit through climactic comebacks. So when the legend was diagnosed with the disease he dubbed "the Big C" in 1964, most were quick to acknowledge cancer may have met its match.

John Wayne's first bout with cancer began when doctors found a tumor the size of a golf ball on his left lung. At the time, the myriad health risks associated with smoking cigarettes were far less known than they are today, and Duke

was one of many Hollywood stars who casually burned through a pack in a day. The alarming discovery of the cancerous mass left John Wayne with no other option but to have it—along with two of his ribs—surgically removed. The risky procedure was a success; and naturally, the star refused to let the loss of an organ and some bones slow him down too much.

Duke was back on his feet in no time following the procedure, though he was well aware he couldn't simply move on as if nothing had happened. On December 29, 1964—just two months after being discharged from the hospital—John Wayne set the record straight regarding his battle with the deadly disease by holding a press conference in his living room. "They told me to withhold my cancer operation from the public because it would hurt my image," the star told the reporters in attendance. "Isn't there a good image in John Wayne beating cancer? Sure, I licked the Big C."

John Wayne with his wife Pilar and son Ethan on the set of *The Sons of Katie Elder* (1965).

Still, John Wayne could only do so much to keep his tireless career on schedule. When his recovery from surgery briefly put production of his next project *The Sons of Katie Elder* on hold, Duke suggested his friend Kirk Douglas be called on as his replacement in the lead role of John Elder. But as someone who had already known John Wayne for more than two decades since their time together on 1941's *The Shepherd of the Hills*, director Henry Hathaway knew what the star was capable of both on and off screen. A recent cancer survivor himself, Hathaway told Duke to rest up and come to the set when he was ready. Sure enough, John Wayne showed up roughly eight weeks later, ready to work. And knowing Duke was up to the task, Hathaway didn't tone down the physicality the role called for. "Well, old Henry was very thoughtful of me, of course, since I was recuperating and all," John Wayne joked to Roger Ebert in a 1968 interview. "He took me up to 8,500 feet to shoot the damned thing, and the fourth day of shooting he had me jumping into ice water. Very considerate."

When John Wayne entered his second bout with "the Big C"—this time stomach cancer, which would ultimately take his life—he continued to work just as he would have with a clean bill of health. And this time around, the legend chose to be even more forthcoming about his own battle as he furthered his efforts to spread awareness about the illness. In the mid-1970s, Duke filmed a series of PSAs with the American Cancer Society seeking donations. One particularly poignant PSA features John Wayne utilizing a moment from his final film *The Shootist* to emphasize the importance of the organization's work. After rolling the clip of J.B. Books learning he has cancer in his doctor's office, Duke tells viewers, "Before that picture was made, I did the same scene in real life."

From left: Earl Holliman, Dean Martin, John Wayne and Michael Anderson Jr. in *The Sons of Katie Elder* (1965).

By choosing to acknowledge his cancer even when others warned it could tarnish his image, John Wayne was empowering not only himself, but also anyone else facing a similar battle. Calling it "the Big C" put the power in the hands of those affected, allowing discussions of the disease to occur more

readily without the need to tiptoe around the topic. In fact, the star's daughter Aissa later said the living room press conference was the only time she could recall her father using the term "cancer."

After he lost his life following a 15-year battle with the disease, John Wayne's family decided to honor their beloved Duke by founding the John Wayne Cancer Foundation as well as the John Wayne Cancer Institute, which has been carrying on the actor's legacy of resilience by helping individuals around the world courageously bring the fight to "the Big C."

★ JESSE OWENS ★

BORN IN ALABAMA in 1913, as the youngest of a poor African American farming family's 10 children, Jesse Owens learned to overcome insurmountable odds before he'd even entered kindergarten. Just after his fifth birthday, Owens developed a painful bump on his chest that began pressing into his lungs. Without enough money to summon a doctor for a house call, the family was forced to improvise. His mother sterilized a knife over an open flame, then cut out the golf ball-sized fibrous tumor from her son's body. Despite losing a great deal of blood, the boy pulled through, and the Owens family left the segregated south to find better paying jobs in the north, settling in Cleveland, Ohio.

While working odd jobs to support himself during junior high, Owens discovered his love of running, waking up early to practice laps at the school track before heading to class; by high school, he was competing in national track competitions. Before long, Owens's father found work at Ohio State University, and despite not having received a scholarship to study, Owens had found a way in, keeping up with his side jobs as he enrolled at the school full-time. Known as the "Buckeye Bullet," the gifted track and field star racked up eight National Collegiate Athletic Association championships between 1935 and 1936 and even set three world records in the long jump, the sprint and the 220-meter

low jump hurdles. But to Owens's growing frustration, the racism he thought he'd left behind in the south still had a home in the north. Forced to live off-campus in "blacks-only" accommodations, more humiliations followed when he was forced to find "blacks-only" hotels and restaurants while traveling on the road with the track team.

In 1936, Owens got the chance of a lifetime to participate in the Olympic Games. Leaders from the National Association for the Advancement of Colored People attempted to dissuade him from attending, pointing out that the leader of the Games' host country, Adolf Hitler, was a fanatical eugenicist bent on creating a superior Aryan race, and that attending such an event could be seen as an endorsement of his country's racist regime. Yet Owens remained steadfast in his desire to prove Hitler's race theory wrong by shining on the global stage.

Traveling to Berlin, the talented African American track star made a sensation in the heart of the Third Reich, outrunning the competition to thunderous applause again and again. He took home not one, not two, but a whopping four gold medals in the 100-meter dash, the 200-meter sprint, the long jump and the 4x100-meter relay, a record that went untouched for 48 years. Just when the Nazis had all eyes on their Third Reich, Owens's victory foiled Hitler's carefully orchestrated PR stunt, flipping the script on those who attempted to define a "superior race."

CHIEF STANDING ★ BEAR ★

THROUGHOUT HISTORY, STRUGGLES for social and civil rights have taken people of intense resilience to lead them. When one segment of society loudly proclaims that another isn't worthy of being considered equal, it is much easier to go along with those who yell the loudest than those who firmly demand to be treated with dignity by law. When modern readers think of such people, the most obvious example is Dr. Martin Luther King Jr. (see page 200), but almost a century before King's assassination, a Chief of the Ponca Nation named Standing Bear initiated a landmark decision that guaranteed civil rights for Native Americans.

As the United States was pushing toward the Pacific Ocean in its mad dash toward Manifest Destiny, the government disregarded the needs of the native population of the Western U.S. The majority of tribes were sent to reservations in present-day Oklahoma, a process that was largely possible because the right of Habeas Corpus was only extended to white Americans, allowing Native Americans to be detained on reservations with no lawful recourse. Until, that is, Standing Bear challenged the practice in court,

essentially forcing the U.S. government to admit that American Indians were human beings and thus, deserved the right of Habeas Corpus.

GEORGE ★ WASHINGTON ★

T O MODERN AMERICANS, the events of December 19, 1777, are unthinkable: the capital city, Philadelphia, had been captured, leaving 12,000 soldiers and 400 women and children unwilling or unable to live under British occupation without a home. In the freezing cold, they marched to Valley Forge, Pennsylvania, and made a crude settlement there consisting of 1,500 log huts. The Continental Army dug in to protect the countryside from this encampment that was, according to the National Parks Service, the fourth largest city in the country at the time. Without enough food or supplies to last the winter, they turned to their commander, General George Washington for guidance.

We remember Washington as an almost mythic figure in the founding of our nation today, but for those thousands at Valley Forge, he was very real—and the one thing standing between the very real prospects of life and death. It's unlikely that history will provide proof of his cutting down a cherry tree and being honest about it, but his leadership at Valley Forge proved before there even was a United States that his integrity and resilience would help define it. With the power of his personality he kept morale from slipping, and with the power of his pen, he persuaded the Congress to reform the supply system threatening to starve his people. He is, in other words, the kind of legendary leader whom we should strive to emulate for generations to come.

★ DAVID GOGGINS ★

PETTY OFFICER 1ST Class David Goggins was living paycheck to paycheck as a night-shift exterminator. Though he'd spent five years in the Air Force, the 24-year-old had let his training go by the wayside and weighed close to 300 pounds. After hearing a television ad for the Navy SEALs, Goggins decided he was ready for a radical change, saying, "I got sick of being haunted by being nobody." When a recruitment officer informed him he'd need to meet the maximum weight requirement of 191 pounds, Goggins shed 100 pounds in 59 days.

To complete his SEAL training, though, Goggins had to make it through Hell Week, a grueling five days and five nights of continuous training. Despite suffering a hernia and bouts of pneumonia on his first two attempts, Goggins passed his third Hell Week with flying colors. In 2001, he joined SEAL Team 5 and saw active duty in Iraq. By 2004, he'd graduated with distinction

from the Army Ranger School. But the following year, when Goggins learned all but one of the members of SEAL Team 10 had been killed by Taliban militants in Operation Red Wings, he began running ultramarathons to raise money for the Special Operations Warrior Foundation; to date, he's raised more than $2 million. In 2013, he set a Guinness world record by completing 4,020 pull-ups in 17 hours. By relentlessly pushing the limits of his body in the name of helping others, Goggins epitomizes the indefatigable power of the human spirit.

★ ULYSSES S. GRANT ★

YEARS BEFORE HE led the Union Army against the Confederacy or served as the 18th President of the United States, Ulysses S. Grant's devotion to his country inspired him to boldly carry on in the face of certain death. Born in 1822 in Point Pleasant, Ohio, by 21, Grant had graduated from West Point, where he demonstrated considerable skill as an equestrian. But before he could settle down and marry his sweetheart, Grant received orders to depart to Mexico, where the U.S. had just declared war against the forces of Gen. Antonio López de Santa Anna.

Fighting under the direction of future president Maj. Gen. Zachary Taylor, Grant put his horsemanship to good use at the Battle of Monterrey. After volunteering to find more ammunition, he took off at full gallop, dodging enemy gunfire by dangling sideways off his horse as mortars bombarded the plaza around him. As a First Lieutenant, during the crucial Battle for Mexico City, he directed his unit to assemble a howitzer gun atop a church and open fire on Gen. Santa Anna's troops, paving the way for an expedited U.S. victory.

Grant returned to Missouri and married his love. But just before the birth of his second child, duty called Grant to sail with the 4th infantry regiment from New York City to Panama and on to California. The trip proved perilous, as Grant arrived in the town of Colón at the height of a severe cholera epidemic. The mules that had been hired to carry them across the jungles never arrived. Trapped on the outskirts of the jungle, the disease quickly ravaged his men. "About one-third of the [more than 700] people

with me died," Grant later recalled.

He traveled to Panama City, where he founded a field hospital and sent the seriously il to a makeshift quarantine a mile offshore. When nurses refused to touch the ailing patients, Gran began nursing them himself as best as he could.

Grant soon arranged to buy mules to complete the crossing, remaining steely-eyed in his dealings as locals tried to turn a profit off desperate travelers in a health crisis. A few weeks later, he and his men sailed to California.

The horrors he witnessed in Panama stayed with Grant for the rest of his life. Years later, in his first presidential address to Congress, he outlined the need for a canal to link the Atlantic and Pacific Oceans, thereby negating the necessity of overland travel and preventing further loss of life.

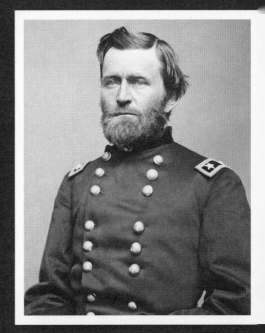

★ BRUCE LEE ★

THE FOURTH CHILD of Lee Hoi Chuen and Grace Ho, Bruce Lee was born at Chinese Hospital in San Francisco, while his father was touring the States as a singer with the Cantonese Opera Company. Today, a plaque at the Chinatown hospital entrance commemorates the newborn's birth. Following in the footsteps of his father, Lee made his acting debut in San Francisco at 3 months old when his father carried the infant while appearing in the 1941 film *Golden Gate Girl*. Before his first birthday, Lee returned to Japanese-occupied Hong Kong with his parents, where they suffered under the brutal regime's rule.

As an adult, when Bruce Lee was trying to make a name for himself in American cinema, he was told over and over again there would never be a Chinese leading man in a Hollywood movie. But Lee didn't consider this a loss—at least, not his loss. Lee maintained confidence in himself and pointed his tireless work ethic in the direction of becoming a superstar.

Briefly discouraged after a string of supporting roles with no hope of a starring one, Lee left America to visit Hong Kong with his 5-year-old son, Brandon, and to arrange for his elderly mother's move to the United States. He was shocked to learn he was a star throughout Asia, thanks to the local popularity of his supporting role as Kato in *The Green Hornet*, which was marketed in Hong Kong as *The Kato Show* years after the series had gone off the air in the U.S.

He soon received an offer from the Hong Kong film studio Golden Harvest to star in two films titled *The Big Boss* and *Fist of Fury* (known as *The Chinese Connection* in the U.S.), respectively. "Chow [owner of Golden Harvest] appeared to me a man of insight and his Golden Harvest Ltd. a promising enterprise," Lee said according to John Little's *Bruce Lee: The Celebrated Life of the Golden Dragon*. "They were, as a company, utilizing practical and efficient methods to promote the ideal of a better film industry, like encouraging independent productions, giving freedom to directors and actors to explore and manifest their talents." And when Lee returned to the U.S. after these films were released he returned as a phenomenon. With hard work and stubborn persistence, he had done the "impossible."

★ WYATT EARP ★

N THE 1920s, before John Wayne fully established the standard for the cinematic cowboy, the spirit of the Western genre was still being configured by filmmakers. At the time, Duke was a mere propman and occasional extra for John Ford, one such director who was determined to bring authenticity to his films. In an effort to do so, Ford invited a living legend to his set: Wyatt Earp.

By the age of 32 in 1880, Earp had carved out a reputation as a no-nonsense lawman in Dodge City, Kansas, the "Wickedest Little City in the West," and Tombstone, Arizona, a silver mining boom town whose citizens settled their disagreements with guns. He counted John "Doc" Holliday among his closest friends, explored much of the western frontier and emerged unscathed and victorious in the infamous gunfight at the O.K. Corral. While the famed former marshal and the young prop worker were generations apart and seemingly disparate at the time of their meeting in 1928, Duke's cinematic career and persona would eventually mirror Earp's incredible life. Fortuitously, the two became friendly between takes, and the 21-year-old eagerly absorbed the legend's recollections and musings.

The wisdom gleaned from those interactions would manifest throughout Duke's career—the star would reflect Earp's last-resort stance on firearm use in films such as *Angel and the Badman* (1947) with the line, "Only a man who carries a gun ever needs one," as well as *True Grit* (1969) when Rooster Cogburn insists, "I never shot nobody I didn't have to." "Earp was the man who had actually done the things in his life that I was trying to do in a movie," Duke once said. Wyatt Earp was the premier icon of the Old West, and John Wayne succeeded in living up to the standards he set.

★ BETHANY HAMILTON ★

AS A YOUNG girl growing up in Hawaii, Bethany Hamilton wanted nothing more than to become a professional surfer. At just 8 years old, she won her first surf contest, and by 12, Hamilton had earned a place as a rising star on the amateur surf scene. But all that progress came to a terrifying halt on October 31, 2003, when a 14-foot-long tiger shark bit off Hamilton's left arm just below the shoulder. By the time she was taken to the hospital, the 13-year-old had lost 60 percent of her blood, sending her body straight into shock. Doctors managed to save Hamilton, but as she recovered, one looming question remained: would she ever surf again?

It was never a question of nerve. Less than a month later, still wearing her bandage, Hamilton decided the only way to be sure she could surf was to get out into the water. She hopped back on her board and did her best to paddle out. Despite having some difficulty in terms of balance, by her third try, Hamilton succeeded in riding a wave into shore. With the full support of her family, Hamilton learned how to surf again on a custom board that her father fitted with a handle, making it easier to maneuver. She released a book about her incredible ordeal, *Soul Surfer: A True Story of Faith, Family, and Fighting to Get Back on the Board*, and in 2005, Hamilton took home first place at a national surf competition. At 17, Hamilton realized her childhood dream by going pro. Four years later, her incredible story was adapted into the 2011 film *Soul Surfer*. And in 2017, the unbreakable top-ranked surfer was inducted into the Surfers' Hall of Fame.

MARGARET
★ CHASE SMITH ★

WHEN MARGARET CHASE Smith's husband lay dying from a heart attack in 1940, he asked her to run for his seat in the U.S. House of Representatives in the upcoming election. With six years of experience on the Maine Republican State Committee already under her belt, Mrs. Smith was hardly a greenhorn when it came to navigating the realm of politics. Having served as her husband's secretary for four years in the nation's capital, she had pored over plenty of internal correspondence, managed his affairs and even written his speeches, gaining an intimate understanding of what being a public servant truly entailed.

Months later, the widowed Smith fulfilled her husband's dying wish and rose to the challenge, becoming the first woman to represent Maine in Congress. When Smith was assigned to the House Naval Affairs Committee in 1943, the politician was tasked with investigating the manufacturing of battleships. Rather than stay behind in D.C. at a time when memories of the carnage at Pearl Harbor remained pronounced, Smith threw herself into the middle of the fray, boldly embarking on a 25,000-mile tour of U.S. naval bases in the South Pacific.

Back on the home front, despite facing a barrage of attacks on the basis of her gender, Smith remained focused on the duties of her office, passing the Women's Armed Forces Integration Act in 1948. She reminded Americans concerned about communist sympathies in the government that every citizen was entitled to "the right to criticize; the right to hold unpopular beliefs; the right to protest; the right of independent thought." Her steadfastness in the face of bigotry and smear campaigns paved the way for more women to serve their country in office.

FREKERICK ★ DOUGLASS ★

IN MARYLAND IN 1818, men like Frederick Douglass were born with absolutely nothing—not even the life, liberty and happiness promised by the founders of the nation. Douglass never knew his real birthday, choosing later in life to celebrate it on Valentine's Day. He was taken away from his mother as a baby, remembering later "My mother and I were separated when I was but an infant ...I do not recollect of ever seeing my mother by the light of day. ... She would lie down with me, and get me to sleep, but long before I waked she was gone." One of the greatest minds of the 19th century, whose pen helped modernize our culture, was born as property. To gain even a shred of human dignity, men like Frederick Douglass had to get out of the South, an act of courage so extreme it proved suicidal for many who tried.

Through a rare lucky turn of fate, Douglass ended up in Baltimore as a boy, where he would later say that compared to plantation life, the city was almost like being free. He began learning the alphabet at 12, but this education soon ended thanks to the draconian views of his master, Thomas Auld, on literacy. Douglass was undeterred, though, and was soon able to read and write well enough that he could teach other slaves to do the same, as well as to study the bible. At 16 he was sent back to plantation life, where he continued his education and began making plans to make a break for freedom. On September 3, 1838, he boarded a northbound train dressed in a sailor's uniform given to him by Anna Murray,

a free woman with whom he had fallen in love. His first free port of call was Philadelphia, and from there he continued to a safe house in New York. Douglass's long wait for freedom was over. But his work was just starting.

Rather than revel in his own freedom, Douglass sent for his wife to join him in New York, then dedicated the rest of his life to using his freedom and literacy to advocate for those who had neither. Murray and Douglass settled in the whaling town of New Bedford, Massachusetts, where he became a licensed preacher in 1839 and honed the oratorical skills that would make him a legend of the abolition movement. By the time the Civil War ended, Douglass was the highest-profile member of America's black community by far, even delivering the keynote address at the unveiling of Washington's Emancipation Memorial. And it was all possible because he refused to give up in his quest for justice.

★ SIDNEY POITIER ★

BORN PREMATURELY IN Miami to parents who were there to sell tomatoes, Sidney Poitier had not been expected to survive infancy. Growing up poor in the Bahamas, the future Oscar-winning actor dropped out of school to help financially support his family by enduring backbreaking labor in a warehouse. By 14, he developed varicose veins in his legs.

With only an elementary school education, the teenager left Nassau and relocated to Florida to make a living while staying with his brother's family. Unfamiliar with racism, Poitier did not grasp the limits of his social standing as an African American in the segregated South. While working as a home delivery boy for a department store, Poitier was repeatedly asked to drop off packages through separate side entrances, and he staunchly refused to take the verbal abuse of those who tried to make him feel inferior. One night, when Poitier returned to his brother's house, his terrified sister-in-law yanked him inside. The Ku Klux Klan had come by, asking for the outspoken teenager.

No longer safe in Florida and with just $39 to his name, the teenager hopped freight trains north to New York City, where he found work as a dishwasher. A kind waiter spent weeks teaching him how to read better, and soon after, Poitier worked as a custodian at the American Negro Theater in exchange for acting lessons. He later drew upon his personal experiences with racial prejudice while portraying an array of complex characters in *No Way Out* (1950), *Blackboard Jungle* (1955), *The Defiant Ones* (1958), *In the Heat of the Night* (1967), *Guess Who's Coming to Dinner* (1967) and more, including *Lilies of the Field* (1963), for which he won an Academy Award for Best Actor—the first ever for an African American.

★ YAKIMA CANUTT ★

ON THE SET of the crime serial *The Shadow of the Eagle* in 1932, an up-and-coming actor named John Wayne would meet Yakima Canutt, who had been hired to play a henchman named Boyle and, perhaps more importantly, serve as the actor's stunt double. Aside from the obvious physical similarities—Canutt was of a similarly imposing stature to Duke, standing about 6'3"—the two men quickly discovered their shared affinity for tomfoolery. Shortly after being introduced to the man hired as his stunt double, Duke was told by fellow actor Bud Osborne that Canutt's true role on set was to serve as a secret spy for one of the producers. Committed to convincing John Wayne the joke was legitimate, Canutt would follow the star of the serial around the set making notes of his every move in a notebook. Eventually, Duke got tired of being spied on, or so he thought, and nearly went after the stuntman. When Osborne revealed it was all a ruse, John Wayne found the whole thing hilarious and formed a fondness for his would-be shadow.

The two men continued to work together on lesser-seen Westerns such as *The Telegraph Trail* (1933) and *Paradise Canyon* (1935), building a friendship as they continued to find common ground. Like Duke, Canutt had a humble upbringing on the west coast, and much of his on-screen authenticity came from spending his younger years working on the family ranch and riding in rodeos. But the stunt actor's rugged cowboy qualities weren't just called upon when the cameras were rolling, they were simply a part of his DNA. And John Wayne, at the time still a young student of the acting game, was eager to absorb anything he could that might help him hone his craft. While observing Canutt dealing with rowdy wranglers and stuntmen on set, Duke discovered the source of some of the inspiration for his iconic persona. Canutt's straight-talking, no-nonsense demeanor made a deep impression on Duke, who admired his friend's steely focus and unwavering resolve under pressure, attributes that John Wayne would later embody with his own signature physicality.

While Canutt never gained fame as an actor in his own right, his contributions to cinema earned him an honorary Academy Award in 1967. Steven Spielberg later paid homage to Canutt's masterful stunts from *Stagecoach* (1939) in his 1981 film *Raiders of the Lost Ark* by having his titular hero, Indiana Jones, slide underneath a racing truck, echoing a scene in which Canutt slides underneath a wagon. The hard work he put in with Duke gave the Western genre the hard-hitting realism it needed to become America's favorite for decades. And what's more, John Wayne's iconic onscreen persona was, according to Duke himself, based on his friend Canutt—a man who always knew the value of putting in the work.

John Wayne and Yakima Canutt go head-to-head in *Wyoming Outlaw* (1939). Among other techniques, Canutt taught Duke how to fall off a horse.

★ NELLIE BLY ★

WHEN NELLIE BLY set her mind to something, there was little she couldn't do. As a teenager, the feisty future author happened upon an article in the *Pittsburgh Dispatch* that espoused how women were only good for giving birth to children and keeping house. Incensed, she quickly penned a letter to the newspaper's editor, giving them a well-worded piece of her mind. To her surprise, the editor not only ran the impassioned reply from the "Lonely Orphan Girl" in his paper—he offered her a full-time job, and she happily accepted.

But when the ambitious young woman's investigative reporting on appalling working conditions in local factories attracted a great deal of negative attention from disgruntled businessmen, she was reassigned, and started writing women's lifestyle pieces on fashion, gardening and other light fare. This did not sit well with Bly who, determined to "do something no girl has done before," set out for Mexico to become a foreign correspondent, sending back dispatches in which she described the everyday lives of ordinary Mexicans under the dictatorial rule of President Porfirio Díaz. Mexican authorities caught wind of the American woman writing negatively of their government in their midst; when they threatened to arrest her, Bly fled the country. Safely squared away back home, she accused Díaz of controlling the press. But despite the quality of her writing, her editor remained unimpressed with Bly's daring adventure. Rather than go back to writing about housekeeping, Bly made the bold decision to quit her job and soon relocated to New York.

Completely broke, the 23-year-old approached Joseph Pulitzer at the *New York World* and persuaded him to take her onboard. Dedicated to going the extra mile, she proposed a daring plan to go undercover at the Women's Lunatic Asylum on Blackwell's Island for what was sure to be a massive story. With no guarantee of her safety or freedom at the end of her 10-day stint, within days, Bly found her way to a women's boarding house, where she accused those around her of being crazy and continuously asked for her "missing trunks." The women immediately became suspicious of Bly and called the police; after a judge deemed her insane, the undercover journalist was whisked away to Blackwell's Island.

Made to wear moth-eaten shawls, sit on hard wooden benches for hours on end, eat rotten food and take ice-cold baths, Bly reasoned Blackwell would make a healthy woman crack in two months. She watched nurses beat and goad patients into lashing out at each other for sport. But perhaps what profoundly disturbed Bly more than anything was that a number of committed women who did not speak English were otherwise mentally sound. None of the nurses who'd examined them had bothered to speak to them in their native languages. After 10 days, lawyers from the *World* sprung her out, and Bly quickly set to documenting her experiences in a series of reports she later published as *Ten Days in a Mad-House*. In surviving her nightmarish ordeal, Bly's daring efforts shocked readers, prompting a grand jury investigation that led to a series of sweeping reforms in treating the mentally ill.

★ SOJOURNER TRUTH ★

BORN INTO SLAVERY in New York in 1797, Sojourner Truth fought for her own personal freedom and for others to gain theirs as well. While the state of New York enacted a law to abolish slavery in 1799, the Emancipation Act wasn't strictly enforced until 28 years later. During that time, Truth endured physical and sexual abuse at the hand of slave owner John Dumont. She bore five children, one of whom Dumont fathered. After years of hearing promises that she'd soon be freed, Truth took her youngest child and fled, seeking refuge with local abolitionists Isaac and Maria Van Wagenen.

But months later, when Truth learned Dumont illegally sold her son John to work the fields in Alabama, the former slave took her fight for justice to the courts. With support from the Van Wagenens, she pled her case before a judge. Incredibly, after several months, the court ruled in Truth's favor and ordered Dumont to return the boy to his mother, making her the first African American to win a lawsuit against a white man. A spiritual awakening led Truth to travel the country spreading the word about the evils of slavery, and despite never having learned how to read or write, she captivated audiences with her incredible gift for rhetoric. The unstoppable emancipated woman advocated for women's suffrage, and during the Civil War, she urged black men to join the Union Army. Living well into her 80s, Truth proved that not even the abhorrent injustice of slavery could break her indomitable spirit.

★ HUGH GLASS ★

BORN IN 1783, Hugh Glass made his living as a frontiersman in the northern reaches of the Louisiana Territory, trapping beaver and engaging in the occasional skirmish with hostile Arikara Native Americans. While accompanying a fur-trading expedition in 1823, he stumbled upon a mother grizzly and her two cubs. The startled animal charged Glass, biting, slashing and crushing his body. Hearing the commotion, his party rushed over to shoot the bear and drag the half-dead man to safety, but with such severe lacerations, the hunters figured he was as good as dead. Wanting to avoid another deadly encounter with the roaming Arikara, the leader of the expedition assigned two men, one of whom was John Fitzgerald, to stay back, await the inevitable, then give him a proper burial. Only they didn't.

When Glass regained consciousness, he found himself wrapped in a bear pelt shroud. Stripped of his favorite rifle and furious at having been left for dead, he set his broken leg and willed himself to crawl and limp more than 200 miles, scavenging for berries, roots, insects, snakes and even animal carcasses. On the last stretch of the six-week journey, he bought a raft from the friendly Lakota tribe and floated down the Missouri River to Fort Kiowa, where he recuperated and learned Fitzgerald had joined the Army. Determined to exact his vengeance, Glass tracked him down to Fort Atkinson, but discovered he would not be permitted to fight Fitzgerald; the Army would not allow a civilian to attack a soldier. The details remain sketchy—whether the enlisted man gave it up begrudgingly or on an order—but Glass finally dropped the matter after taking back his beloved gun.

ZORA NEALE ★ HURSTON ★

BORN IN 1891 in Notasulga, Alabama, Zora Neale Hurston moved with her family to Eatonville, Florida, when she was 3 years old. Just six miles north of Orlando, the town of Eatonville took pride in being the oldest African American city in the U.S., an accolade it continues to enjoy in the 21st century. But during Hurston's lifetime, Eatonville provided a safe oasis of black culture in the Jim Crow south. She described it as a "city of five lakes, three croquet courts, three hundred brown skins, three hundred good swimmers, plenty guavas, two schools, and no jailhouse." Living in a town built on black pride rather than suffering instilled Hurston with an immutable confidence, an insatiable drive and joy for exploring her roots.

As the daughter of former slaves, Hurston worked as a maid to an actor in a traveling Gilbert & Sullivan group, earning money to support herself through high school. She attended the historically all-black Howard University and earned a scholarship to study at Barnard College. Hurston flourished in the New York City art and literary scenes. Arriving at the height of the Harlem Renaissance, she soon became acquainted with noted black luminaries such as W.E.B. DuBois, collaborating with Langston Hughes and Countee Cullen and launching a short-lived literary magazine called *Fire!!*

While studying at Barnard, Hurston had the opportunity to meet the famed anthropologist Franz Boas, who inspired the budding writer to document the African American traditions of the South. She threw herself into studying slave songs, traditions and other bits of folklore, traveling to Alabama, Georgia, Haiti and Jamaica. Incredibly, she located and interviewed the last living survivor of the last slave ship to arrive in the U.S., Cudjo Lewis, eager to preserve his story for future generations.

In 1937, she published her best-known work, *Their Eyes Were Watching God*. Hurston drew upon the memories of her beloved Eatonville to provide the setting for her liberated female protagonist, an African American woman named Janie who, over the course of a series of relationships, finally defies the gender norms imposed on her by her lovers to tragic results, gaining her own freedom in the process.

Despite the beauty of her unpretentious prose, this seminal work put Hurston at odds with the agenda of the black elite, who found her depictions of black country life and careful use of dialect in her writing overly simplistic, immature, foolish and downright offensive. But Hurston paid no mind to their criticism, writing, "I am not tragically colored...I do not weep at the world—I'm too busy sharpening my oyster knife." Not unlike her character, Hurston drew her strength from defying others' expectations, daring to "have the nerve to walk my own way, however hard, in my search for reality, rather than climb upon the rattling wagon of wishful illusions." ·

★ DOLLY PARTON ★

ONG BEFORE HER days as a rhinestone-studded superstar, Dolly Parton grew up dirt poor, one of 12 children living in a cramped woods Tennessee mountain cabin with ectricity and no indoor plumbing. In ummers, the Partons would head out ocal river to wash themselves with made soap, and when winter came, ime meant passing around a tin pan with water. Having barely any money rape together forced the Parton family d creative solutions to their everyday ems, and one year, Dolly's mother e her daughter a coat out of various s of fabric she was able to scrounge so oung girl would have something warm to wear in the coming cold months. As s developed her musical talents by perform live on local radio stations, and later making her Grand Ole Opry debut at just 13, Dolly drew on the circumstances of h hardscrabble childhood to provide color backgrounds for her growing catalogue songs. Four years after releasing her de solo album, she commemorated her hum beginnings in the 1971 hit track "Coat of Many Colors," an ode to her family. Out of more than 3,000 songs, she still cites this one as her favorite—a deeply person reminder that her truly remarkable, litera rags-to-riches story was made possible through the values espoused by her love ones. As the song she wrote goes, "One only poor, only if they choose to be."

★ ROCKY MARCIANO ★

BEFORE THE LIKES of Muhammad Ali or Floyd Mayweather, Rocky Marciano captivated American audiences with his unrelenting drive to pummel the competition. Born to Italian immigrants in Brockton, Massachusetts, in 1923, the future heavyweight champ developed the will to fight early in life after contracting pneumonia at just 18 months old. The tiny toddler pulled through, and as a teenager, Marciano fashioned his own weightlifting equipment, hanging a stuffed mailsack from a tree in his backyard to use as a punching bag. He further developed his athletic abilities on his school's football and baseball teams before dropping out at the end of his sophomore year.

In 1943, Marciano was drafted into service in the Army, where he helped ferry supplies across the English Channel to Normandy. While waiting for his discharge after the war's end, Marciano participated in amateur fights, even winning the 1946 Amateur Armed Forces boxing tournament.

Making his return to civilian life, Marciano could no longer resist his boyhood dream of becoming a baseball legend and tried out for a farm team of the Chicago Cubs. But despite his best efforts, he failed to land a spot. After coming home, he fully devoted himself to becoming a boxer, running at least seven miles a day. He ended his first professional match in 1947 by knocking out his opponent, Lee Epperson, in the third round, and went on to win the next 15 matches in similar fashion.

At almost 25 years old and weighing close to 190 pounds, the short, clumsy heavyweight

was considered too light, too slow and too old to make much of a career out of fighting. But Marciano's monk-like focus—paired with the help of professional trainer Charley Goldman—gave him the ability to outlast any opponent and roll with the punches.

On October 26, 1951, Marciano knocked out former heavyweight champ Joe Louis, taking him down in the eighth round. Eleven months later, he took home the heavyweight crown after going head-to-head with "Jersey Joe" Walcott with an incredible KO punch in the 13th round. The "Brockton Blockbuster" managed to defend his title for another five fights, capping off his career with a bout against Archie Moore on September 21, 1955, who went down after a ninth-round knockout.

On April 27, 1956, at 31, the powerhouse pugilist hung up his gloves for good to spend more time with family. Over the course of 49 fights, no one ever managed to beat Marciano, and he finished his career undefeated, inspiring real life boxers as well as fictional ones—namely Rocky Balboa.

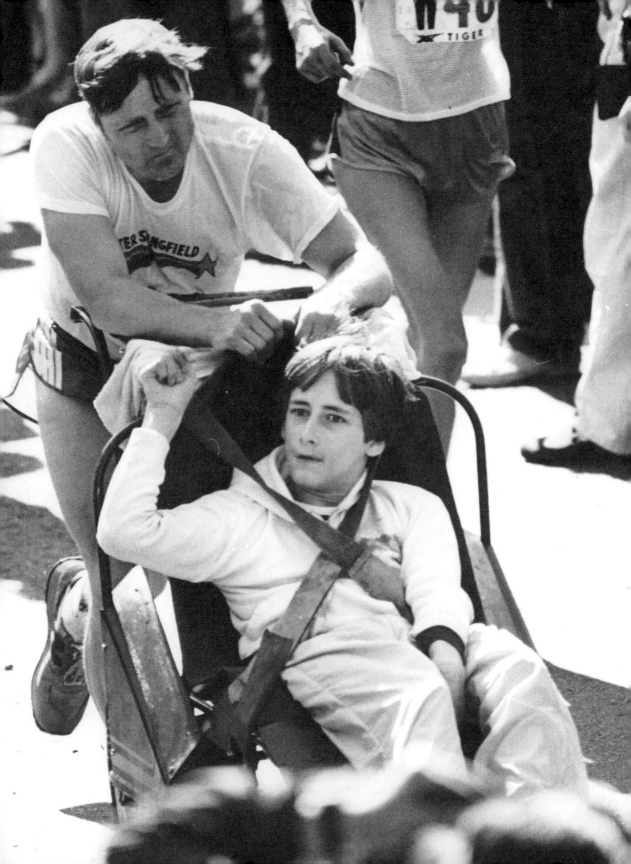

★ "TEAM HOYT" ★

OCTORS FIGURED THAT Rick Hoyt would not have much quality of life. Born as a spastic quadriplegic with cerebral palsy, Rick's body would never allow him to walk or speak, and medical professionals deemed him little more than a vegetable. But Dick and Judy Hoyt noticed their son's eyes would still track them as they moved around a room, and this inspired them to take him to Boston Children's Hospital, where a specialist advised the Hoyts to treat Rick no differently than they would their other children.

At home, Dick and Judy raised Rick like any other child—taking him on family vacations, encouraging him to play sports with his siblings and helping him learn basic words. In fact, Judy managed to teach Rick the alphabet by cutting letters out of sandpaper and labeling objects throughout the house. When public school teachers refused to look beyond their son's physical disabilities, however, the frustrated but undeterred couple called on local legislators to enact change and allow their son the opportunity to obtain an education. In 1972, with help the engineering department at Tufts University, the Hoyts presented their 11-year-old son with a life-changing gift: an interactive computer designed specifically for his use. With it, he could select letters by tapping his head against a part of the machine that had been mounted to his wheelchair. A diehard sports fan, Rick's first words to his parents were, "Go Bruins!"

The Hoyts' fight to allow disabled children the right to an education tailored to fit their unique needs paid off in 1972 with the passing of Massachusetts Chapter 766, the first special education law in the country. Three years later, when Congress approved the Education for All Handicapped Children Act, at 13, Rick was finally allowed into public school.

In 1977, Rick approached his father and informed him he wanted to participate in a 5-mile run to raise money for one of his fellow students who'd been paralyzed in a car accident. Despite not being much of a runner himself, Dick heard his son out and agreed to push Rick in a wheelchair for the duration of the race. They finished all five miles and came in second-to-last, but later that night, Rick confided in his father, "Dad, when I'm running, it feels like I'm not handicapped." Moved by his son's indomitable spirit, Dick began training for more races in earnest by running with a sack of cement in a wheelchair.

As "Team Hoyt," the dynamic father-son duo tackled more than 1,100 endurance races, including Ironman competitions, several Boston Marathons and, in 1992, a 3,735-mile journey across the U.S. by bike and on foot—a feat they completed in just 45 days. After several decades of racing, Team Hoyt prepared to cap off their long career by participating in the 2013 Boston Marathon. But when a terrorist act disrupted the race, the dedicated team decided to come back and finish the next year's race "Boston Strong." With the support of his family, Rick refused to let his condition stop him from striving for greatness.

★ BILLIE JEAN KING ★

I N 1973, Billie Jean King was the perfect opponent for Bobby Riggs, a retired men's tennis pro who bragged he could beat any of the game's top women, even at 55. An advocate for women's rights who once led a walk-out when the Pacific Southwest Tennis Tournament offered female competitors just 15 percent of the prize money it offered the men, despite equal ticket sales, King initially refused to play against him. However, after he bested Margaret Court using a series of drop shots and lobs and continued to egg on King, calling himself a "woman specialist," the 29-year-old King decided to engage. The game, a televised, winner-take-all competition for $100,000, quickly became known as the Battle of the Sexes. And the press tour sealed it, with Riggs preening and prodding with sexist statements including: "I'll tell you why I'll win. She's a woman, and they don't have the emotional stability." During the match, King made Riggs pay, ever ready for his drop shots and lobs. She won handily in straight sets: 6–4, 6–3, 6–3. After the match, critics complained that the age difference

between the two players played too large a factor, with some wondering whether the whole match had been staged. For his part, Riggs knew the truth, his words, according to King, standing as a small bit of vindication for women everywhere: "I really underestimated you."

COL. BENJAMIN H. ★ VANDERVOORT ★

A S A BOY in Niagara County, New York, and a student at Maryland's Washington College, Benjamin "Vandy" Vandervoort was a standout in several arenas. As a track and football star, member of the drama club and YMCA, and an officer of Theta Chi, he distinguished himself as officer material and was commissioned as soon as he graduated. Two years later in 1940, he proved that collecting skills wasn't something he'd left behind in civilian life by joining the paratroopers, then a newly formed organization. By the time the paratroopers were ready to take Europe, he had been promoted to Major. No one could grind down the iron resilience of Benjamin Vandervoort from Sicily to Salerno and across Italy as his paratroopers helped liberate the peninsula from fascist rule.

His work in Italy was so impressive that the Army promoted him yet again, making him a Lieutenant Colonel before sending him to France as the Commanding Officer of the 2nd Battalion, 505th Parachute Infantry Regiment. On June 6, 1944, Vandervoort parachuted into enemy territory and broke his leg. Committed to neutralizing the Nazi threat, he ordered a medic to tightly lace his boot so he could press on against the German counterattack mowing down American troops on the beaches of Normandy.

In the aftermath of the war in Europe, Vandervoort was made a full Colonel, but another feather in his cap was still to come, albeit not from the Army. When the D-Day invasion was immortalized on film in the 1962 epic war drama *The Longest Day*, John Wayne played Vandervoort, ensuring that everyone who saw the film would remember the Colonel's name.

Duke as Col. Benjamin H. Vandervoort in *The Longest Day* (1962).

★ STEVE MCQUEEN ★

TO REACH THE top of any profession requires an incredible amount of hard work and focus, not to mention an unbreakable spirit and plenty of nerve. For this reason we see many Hollywood success stories prologued by hard times and hard work. While John Wayne's own story is full of both, perhaps no other pre-Hollywood story of hardship compares to that of Duke's acquaintance Steve McQueen. Born to a mother who wasn't ready for him and a father who abandoned her, McQueen was sent away as a small child to live with his grandparents and great-uncle Claude in depression-era Missouri. Here, an ear infection left him partially deaf and he discovered a learning disability that would later reveal itself to be dyslexia. At 8 years old he was taken to Indianapolis to live with his mother and her new husband. Sadly, McQueen's stepfather was abusive, and McQueen soon ran away from home to escape his brutality, living on the street in petty criminality.

Before long, young McQueen was too much of a handful for his mother, who had divorced and married again—to another man who also used his fists liberally on the boy. He moved back to his uncle Claude's for a time, but eventually ran away to rejoin his street gangs, and soon found himself getting arrested for stealing hubcaps. This arrest incensed his stepfather so much he beat McQueen bloody and threw him down a flight of stairs. He persuaded McQueen's mother to send her son to California Junior Boys Republic in Chino, California, a school for "incorrigible" boys. By 16, McQueen was out in the world living as an adult. He followed a stint in the U.S. Merchant Marines by working a series of odd jobs in a brothel, as a lumberjack and as a carnival barker.

In 1947, McQueen finally found a path out of his juvenile life of crime by joining the U.S. Marine Corps, which provided a constructive outlet for his boundless energy and molded his ability to thrive under pressure. During an arctic exercise, he saved five fellow Marines as their tank threatened to crash through ice and into the freezing water below. Once out of the Marines, the G.I. Bill provided McQueen the novel opportunity to pursue what he felt was his calling for the first time. Finally free to do as he pleased, he chose to study acting.

In 1959, a big break came when Frank Sinatra chose McQueen to replace Sammy Davis Jr. in the film *Never So Few*. The following year, McQueen would ride onto the set of *The Magnificent Seven* and into Hollywood immortality. Through sheer will power, McQueen persevered in rising above the circumstances of his abusive childhood to become an American icon of strength and steely resolve.

★ CRAZY HORSE ★

FOR A LONG time, when U.S. school books told the story of the Battle of the Little Bighorn, General George Armstrong Custer was the undisputed hero of the story. With the benefit of hindsight, today we can recognize that while some still cherish the tragic cavalryman, he was not the only military leader of note on

the field that day. In fact, were it not for the martial wherewithal of Chief Crazy Horse, or in Lakota, Tasunke Witko, our history books would read very differently. A warrior since his mid-teens, Crazy Horse was born only a few miles from the South Dakota mountain that now bears his name and an unfinished memorial to his bravery.

Unwilling to accept that his ancestral lands were to be subsumed by westward-traveling American settlers and the U.S. government, Crazy Horse vowed to fight for his way of life, even if that meant using force. He would continue to do so throughout his adulthood, culminating in the 1876 battle at which he prevented Custer's reinforcements from arriving. This victory made him one of the most respected chiefs of the plains, and one the government had no choice but to take seriously. His resilience was so steadfast that when U.S. soldiers attempted to imprison him during peace talks in 1877, he preferred to draw his knife and die fighting to losing his freedom. More than 100 years after his death, Crazy Horse was honored with a U.S. postage stamp bearing his likeness as part of the postal service's Great Americans series.

★ ARON RALSTON ★

ON SATURDAY, APRIL 26, 2003, as mountaineering enthusiast Aron Ralston made his solo descent into a three-foot-wide section of Bluejohn Canyon, an 800-pound boulder shifted, crushing his right hand and wrist. Pinned against the canyon wall, and with no cell phone on hand, the outdoorsman shuddered as it dawned on him that he'd failed to tell anyone about his plans for the day.

Minutes turned to hours. By Tuesday, Ralston had run out of food and water and resorted to drinking his own urine. Unable to put a dent in or otherwise move the boulder, Ralston used his video camera to record his goodbyes. With a cheap multitool, the delirious mountaineer carved his epitaph into the canyon wall and fell asleep. Incredibly, he dreamed of seeing a child running toward a one-armed man. He took the message to heart, and the vision of his future helped steel Ralston to break the bones in his wedged arm.

Fashioning a tourniquet out of his Camelbak water bottle's tubing, he cut off circulation to his arm, then used the multitool to begin cutting through the skin and muscle. A pair of pliers helped him finish off his tendons, and finally, Ralston cut through

his arteries. After climbing out of the canyon and rappelling off a cliff, Ralston ran into a family of hikers, who helped him to safety. His harrowing six-day experience and undying desire to live was adapted for the silver screen in the 2010 film *127 Hours*.

★ ERNEST HEMINGWAY ★

EFORE PUBLISHING groundbreaking works of literature like *For Whom the Bell Tolls* and *The Old Man and the Sea,* Ernest Hemingway cheated death and survived a wide array of ailments to cement his place as one of the greatest authors of all time.

During World War I, while driving ambulances in Italy for the American Red Cross, an 18-year-old Hemingway was distributing cigarettes and chocolates to Italian troops when a mortar shell landed several feet away. One man was killed instantaneously, while another had his legs blown off and died shortly thereafter. After being knocked out by the blast, Hemingway came to, threw another Italian soldier over his shoulder and carried him to safety. He later had an operation to remove more than 200 pieces of shrapnel embedded throughout his legs and spent six months recuperating from his injuries. For his bravery in combat, Hemingway received an aluminum kneecap and the Italian medal of valor, the Croce de Guerra.

But this brush with death only proved the first of many close calls over the course of the author's life. While enjoying a swim on his honeymoon in 1927, Hemingway contracted anthrax. The following year, thinking it was a toilet pull chain, Hemingway yanked down a skylight in his bathroom only to have it crash over his head. The intense pain of this particular accident inspired him to work through the harrowing experiences he endured during the Great War and formed the basis of his 1929 novel, *A Farewell to Arms.*

In World War II, Hemingway and other war correspondents were barred from storming the beaches of Normandy alongside American troops on June 6, 1944. This didn't stop Hemingway from wanting to personally join in the fight. Instead, he made up for having missed out on combat by ripping off the patch on his uniform denoting his status as a member of the press and posed as a member of the infantry on a mission to retake a French village from the Nazis. And while Hemingway was almost court martialed for this brazen behavior, he managed to talk his way out of further trouble by claiming that, as a war veteran, he'd only been there to offer strategic advice.

Ten years after witnessing the D-Day landings, Hemingway survived not one but two back-to-back plane crashes. On a Christmas trip to Africa with his wife Mary, the Hemingways were flying aboard a chartered plane over the Belgian Congo when their aircraft struck a pole and crashed. Hemingway emerged from the wreckage with a head wound, while Mary staggered out with two broken ribs. The next day, during an attempt to seek medical attention, the Hemingways' plane exploded shortly after take-off—the author sustained a concussion and burns so serious, several newspapers reported he died in the ensuing blaze. It seems nothing, whether it be malaria, pneumonia, dysentery, skin cancer, hepatitis, anemia, diabetes, high blood pressure, a ruptured spleen, a fractured skull or dozens of electroshock therapy sessions could persuade Hemingway from living, or ending, life on his terms.

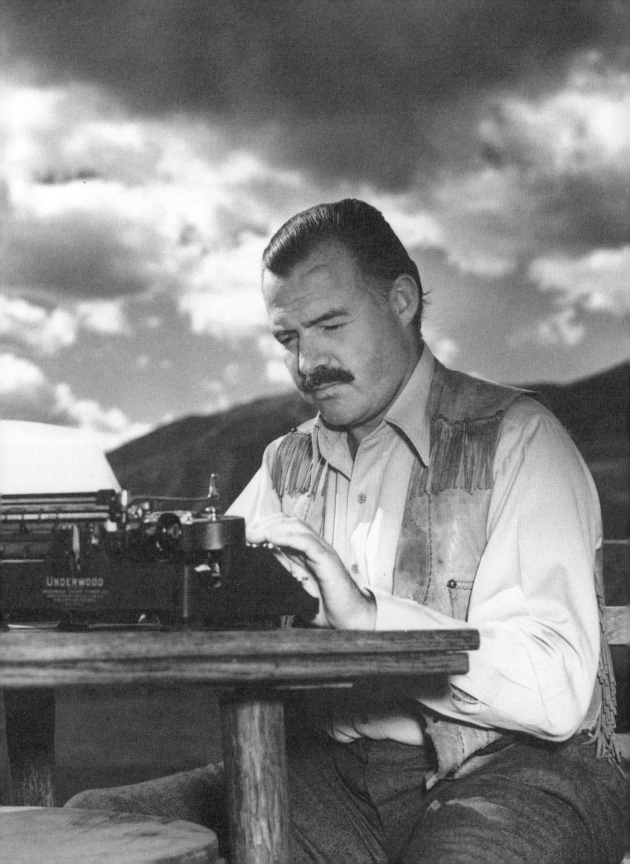

★ COURAGE ★

DUKE HIMSELF SAID IT BEST: "COURAGE IS BEING SCARED TO DEATH BUT SADDLING UP ANYWAY."

John Wayne helms production of *The Green Berets* (1968). Most of the filming took place at Fort Benning near Columbus, Georgia.

STICKING
★ TO HIS GUNS ★

DUKE DEFIED THE STATUS QUO IN HOLLYWOOD TO MAKE A FILM HONORING AMERICA'S TROOPS IN VIETNAM.

AS THE VIETNAM War raged on into the 1960s, the debate over America's involvement intensified. Many in Hollywood were vocal about their opposition to the conflict and used their celebrity as a platform for protest. But John Wayne, whose patriotism only strengthened in times of strife, saw clearly through the partisanship and straight to the heart of the matter: brave, young Americans were risking life and limb in a far-off land, unsure of when—or if—they would return home. Regardless of what his peers in the industry might think, Duke was determined to highlight the heroism of the U.S. troops overseas; and in 1968, he would get the opportunity to do just that by co-directing and starring in *The Green Berets*.

While he was initially inspired by Robin Moore's 1965 book *The Green Berets*, which details the author's

experiences with Special Forces in Vietnam, John Wayne also had his own up-close experience to draw from when envisioning the film. In the summer of 1966, as part of a tour organized by the USO's Hollywood Overseas Committee and the U.S. Department of Defense, the actor spent time getting to know some of the courageous individuals serving on the frontlines of Vietnam. The experience proved more than a technical research opportunity for what would become *The Green Berets*, as the icon also gained plenty of perspective and personal inspiration for the patriotic picture.

The task of creating a film about a still-ongoing conflict would not be one John Wayne would take on without appropriate precaution. Hoping to present as much earnest realism as possible, Duke fearlessly went straight to the top of the pecking order by writing a letter to President Lyndon B. Johnson seeking government approval for the project. "We want to tell the story of our fighting men in Vietnam with reason,

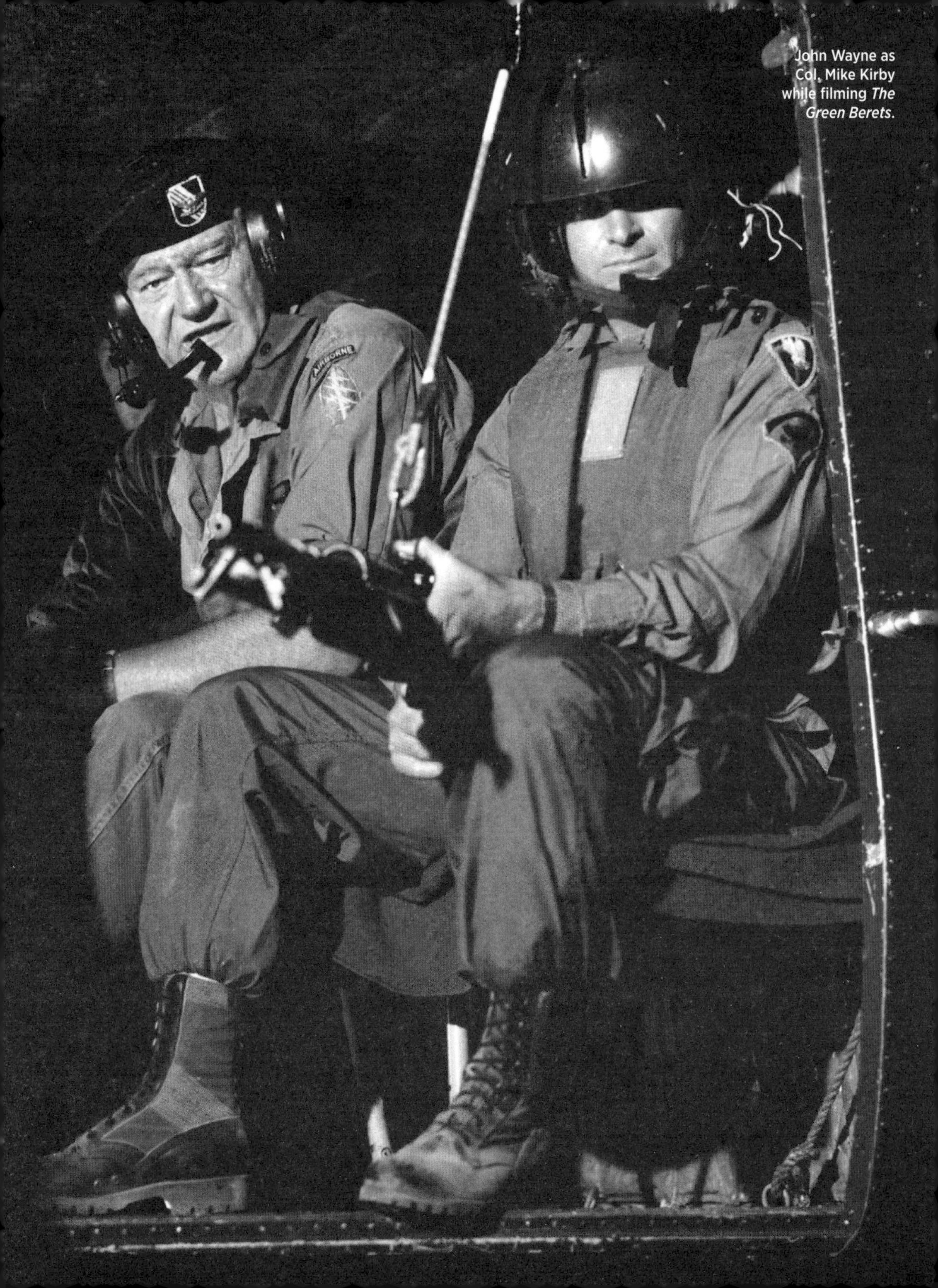

John Wayne as Col. Mike Kirby while filming *The Green Berets*.

emotion, characterization and action," the legend wrote to the 36th President of the United States. "We want to do it in a manner that will inspire a patriotic attitude on the part of fellow-Americans—a feeling which we have always had in this country in the past during times of stress and trouble." Well aware of the star's flag-waving support of the American cause, Johnson's adviser Jack Valenti assured the president that John Wayne was the right man to handle the subject with care. Not only did the commander-in-chief sign off on the idea, but the Pentagon also granted Duke access to numerous personnel, props and military bases through the Pentagon.

Backed by the U.S. government, John Wayne proudly tied himself to production of *The Green Berets*, not only as the film's director, but also its financial backer via his production company Batjac. The majority of the film's exterior scenes—including the Battle of Nam Dong in the film's climax— were shot at the Army post at Fort Benning, Georgia, which Duke further decked-out by dipping deep into the Batjac budget. And when he wasn't busy perfecting the set and directing the action during the production, Duke was donning his own green beret with patriotic pride to play the hardheaded Col. Mike Kirby. As is the case with any of the films in which he plays a member of the Armed Forces, John Wayne's performance in *The Green Berets* beams with strength, conviction and a never-say-die spirit— much like his own path to making the film a reality.

But despite the blessing of the president and the Pentagon and the boosted morale of the men he met overseas, Duke did not receive the same support from critics. Largely focused on the film's perceived politics rather than its performances and

John Wayne walks along a row of troops in a scene from *The Green Berets*.

production value, many were unkind in their reviews of *The Green Berets*. But, ultimately, it didn't matter. Much like Col. Kirby's line to the young war orphan

Hamchunk at the end of the film, *The Green Berets* was the legend's way of telling the troops, "You're what this is all about."

And like those he admired on the battlefield, John Wayne could hang his beret on the fact that he had pushed forward with the project because he believed in the cause: supporting America's brave men in uniform during a time when a lot of his countrymen would not.

★ HARRIET TUBMAN ★

IT WOULD HAVE been gutsy enough if Harriet Tubman had escaped her enslavement and lived to tell her story, but she knew securing her own freedom wasn't enough. Born into slavery during the 1820s, Tubman was rented out by her slave owner to work for neighboring farmers, which kept her painfully isolated from the rest of her family. Although she endured frequent beatings and lashings, Tubman said she never once gave her masters the satisfaction of hearing her "holler" in pain.

As a teenager, while accompanying her current owner's cook into a store to shop for groceries, Tubman witnessed a fellow slave making a break for freedom. An overseer entered—spotting Tubman, he demanded she help him capture the fugitive. Tubman refused, and when he attempted to lob a heavy iron weight at the fleeing runaway, it hit Tubman instead. Bloody and dazed, she received no medical attention but nonetheless returned to work only days later. The painful head injury gave Tubman vivid dreams, terrible headaches, blackouts and seizures. By the time her owner threatened to sell her in 1849, Tubman decided the time was right to make her escape. Of this pivotal moment in her life, she later remarked, "I had reasoned this out in my mind, there was one of two things I had a right to, liberty or death; if I could not have one, I would have the other." Under cover of darkness, she utilized the Underground Railroad's extensive network of safehouses to travel a staggering 90 miles on foot to the Pennsylvania border.

But despite her overwhelming joy, Tubman's thoughts remained with her family back home. Even if it meant being killed, she knew she had to go back for them.

Working under the code name "Moses," Tubman led a jaw-dropping 70 people from bondage over the course of 13 rescue missions, some of whom were her own friends and family, and all at great personal risk. Due to her meticulous planning, Tubman never lost a single person under her care.

Yet even after saving her loved ones, Tubman wasn't quite ready to quit what had become her life's mission. Following the outbreak of the Civil War, she served as a Union Army nurse and spy. Incredibly, Tubman not only helped plan a raid on Confederate troops along the Combahee River in South Carolina—she also led 150 black soldiers in freeing more than 700 slaves during the attack.

In her later years, Tubman dedicated herself to furthering the women's suffrage movement by working with Susan B. Anthony and Emily Howland. By the 1890s, her seizures had worsened, preventing her from being able to sleep. Hoping to remedy the head injury she'd sustained years earlier, the elderly abolitionist underwent brain surgery at Massachusetts General Hospital in Boston. When offered anesthetic, she declined, preferring to bite down on a bullet as she'd witnessed soldiers doing in the war. Not even major surgery could slow her down, and Tubman remained active in abolitionist circles until her passing in 1913.

RUBY NELL ★ BRIDGES ★

HEN WE THINK of courage, there are several images and icons likely to enter our minds as Americans. A lot of them are in the pages of this book—these soldiers, explorers, justice-hungry resisters and more populate our visions of bravery, from winning medals in combat to boldly going where no one had gone before. One thing we don't often think of as far as courage is concerned is the elementary school perfect attendance award. Sure, some people pride themselves on never missing a day, but getting up for school when you don't feel like it doesn't seem to compare to breaching the top of a battle trench or mounting a charge against your enemies. The story of Ruby Nell Bridges proves that heroic courage can come from the most unexpected places if circumstances are dire enough: even a list of six-year-old perfect attendance award winners.

Ruby Nell Bridges was born in September 1954 as the Civil Rights Era was dawning and segregationists were beginning their bitter last stand against equality. By the time she was ready to start first grade in 1960, the pot was beginning to boil over as school after school across the South began desegregating. With the help of the NAACP, Bridges and her family volunteered to make her the first African American student at William Frantz Elementary School in New Orleans. As one of only six black students in her Louisiana district to pass an entrance exam created to determine whether or not she'd be able to compete academically at an all-white school, Ruby endured immediate and brutal bullying, and not just from fellow students. Parents who didn't want their children taught alongside Ruby pulled them out of school, leaving Ruby to be taught one-on-one by the only teacher willing to take her on as a pupil. In a 1997 interview, Bridges said, "Driving up I could see the crowd, but living in New Orleans, I actually thought it was Mardi Gras. There was a large crowd of people outside of the school. They were throwing things and shouting, and that sort of goes on in New Orleans at Mardi Gras."

Now 65 and a committed political activist, Ruby Bridges never once cried as she took her rightful place in the Louisiana public school system. The people screaming at her outside school were many times her age and size, threatening her with hateful words and gestures. One woman even brought a mock-up of a black child in a coffin. Despite all this, Bridges never missed a single day, facing the hate-filled mob week after week. Today, American children of all walks of life fill classrooms across the country thanks in part to the gumption of this 6-year-old hero and the people who supported her.

DWIGHT D. ★ EISENHOWER ★

MOST AMERICANS TODAY have no concept of the courage that went into defeating the Axis powers and stopping the Nazi war machine from achieving world domination. As more veterans and their firsthand accounts of fighting in the war pass out of memory, films like *The Longest Day* (1962) provide a rare glimpse of the outstanding individuals who beat unthinkable odds in bringing the war to a victorious close. One of the legendary men who triumphed that day was General Dwight D. Eisenhower.

Born in 1890, young Eisenhower tore through the history books in his home library, sparking a lifelong interest in military history. While his Mennonite mother's pacifism put her at odds with going to war, she nonetheless allowed her son to pursue his ambitions, and in 1911, Eisenhower enrolled at West Point.

Two years after Eisenhower graduated, the U.S. entered World War I. But by the time Eisenhower's unit was ordered to depart for France, the armistice agreement was signed, and the war ended without Eisenhower ever seeing active combat. Over the next two decades, however, the aspiring soldier rose through the ranks and worked under brilliant generals like John J. Pershing, Douglas MacArthur and George Marshall. In 1942, while heading Operation Torch, Maj. Gen. Eisenhower learned invaluable battle strategies firsthand while accompanying the Allied forces throughout North Africa. The next year, he was appointed Supreme Commander of the Allied Expeditionary Force, a title under which he would plan and execute the Allied invasion of Nazi-occupied Europe.

On the morning of June 6, 1944, despite horrible weather and the problems it posed for the landing, Eisenhower made the call to proceed with storming the beaches of Normandy. Knowing the fate of the free world hung on the courage of the young men about to face certain death, he gave the simple order, "Full victory—nothing else." And though there were plenty of casualties, D-Day proved the Allies' finest hour, turning the tide of the war and paving the way for the liberation of Paris on August 25.

When American troops liberated the Ohrdruf concentration camp in April 1945 and word spread of the horrors they found, Eisenhower insisted on personally visiting the site. Accompanied by Gen. Patton, Eisenhower later recalled, "I felt it my duty to be in a position from then on to testify at first hand about these things in case there ever grew up at home the belief or the assumption that 'the stories of Nazi brutality were just propaganda.'" He then ordered every American GI in the area, as well as the German citizens of a nearby town, to tour Ohrdruf and see the atrocities for themselves. For his bravery and vision both on and off the battlefield, Eisenhower cemented his place in history as one of the most brilliant generals of all time.

★ KATHARINE GRAHAM ★

 S THE DAUGHTER of a major publisher, socialite Katharine Graham paid little mind when her father decided to hand over control of *The Washington Post* to her husband, Philip, as well as his reasoning that "no man should be in the position of working for his wife." Yet when Philip took his own life in 1963, Katharine was forced to step up to the challenge of not only running a major paper, but also keeping her family legacy from falling into ruin. Less than 10 years into her tenure, the Nixon administration successfully barred *The New York Times* from publishing the top-secret Pentagon Papers, which featured unsavory details on America's decision making during the Vietnam War. Knowing her paper would likely face its own lawsuit and a great deal of wrath from the president's allies, Graham courageously made the tough call to continue reporting on the explosive documents. When her fears came to pass, the U.S. Supreme Court ultimately ruled in favor of the *Post* and its rights to inform readers under the First Amendment.

But Graham's role in exposing the corruption of the Nixon administration did not end there. Committed to supporting her dedicated journalists, in 1972, she allowed Carl Bernstein and Bob Woodward to carry on with their investigation of the break-in at the Democratic National Committee Headquarters in Washington, D.C., and its ties to the president's reelection campaign. Even though Nixon's Attorney General threatened she'd "get caught in a big fat wringer" for publishing their findings, Graham maintained her grace under fire, and the story caused a sensation, paving the way for Nixon's resignation in 1974. Despite sexist attacks and smears on her character, Graham never stooped to attacking her detractors—instead, she had the courage to let the facts do the talking for her.

★ JOHN PETER ZENGER ★

DECADES BEFORE ANGRY colonists dumped tea into Boston Harbor, John Peter Zenger made his stand against British tyranny by defying bogus libel laws in court. Born in Germany in 1697, at 13, Zenger and his family left Europe to make their home in New York, where he became a printer's apprentice. As an adult, Zenger opened his own printing press and began publishing a newspaper called the *New York Weekly Journal*. In it he ran anonymous articles that accused the corrupt royal governor, William S. Crosby of rigging elections and other crimes. Crosby had Zenger indicted for seditious libel, even though he hadn't penned any of the articles in question.

His spotless reputation on the line, Zenger hired the most famous lawyer of the day, Andrew Hamilton. As the publisher sat before a judge, Hamilton challenged the governor to prove the charges raised against him were false before uttering the prophetic words, "It is not the cause of one poor printer, but the cause of liberty." Moved by Hamilton's defense, the jury ruled in Zenger's favor, establishing a novel freedom of the press that would lend itself to the fight for American independence yet to come.

★ MINNIE FREEMAN ★

JANUARY 12, 1888, began as an unusually warm winter day in Nebraska, with temperatures soaring into the 40s. Nineteen-year-old Minnie Freeman had been teaching more than a dozen children in her sod schoolhouse when she heard hail pelting the windows. A freak snowstorm struck the area, and as all settlers on the prairie knew, that meant staying indoors and hunkering down for the long haul. As the wind began to howl, the mercury plummeted to a bone-chilling 20 degrees below zero. Freeman knew she and her students would not remain safe for long—even if they had enough coal, most were not adequately dressed to await rescue in subzero temperatures. Then the wind blew the schoolhouse door clear off its hinges. The roof tore away, and Freeman knew it was time to leave.

Grabbing twine from her desk, she hurried to wrap herself and each of her frightened students into a long chain. Holding the youngest in her arms, she ordered the children to follow her into the blizzard to seek shelter elsewhere. "I've never felt such a wind," she said. "It blew the snow so hard that the flakes stung your face like arrows. All you could see ahead of you was a blinding, blowing sheet of snow." After an interminable mile of trudging through the storm, they reached a farmhouse, where they waited out the remainder of the storm. The so-called "Schoolchildren's Blizzard" claimed hundreds of lives, but thanks to Freeman's courage, none of her students were among them.

CHESLEY
★ SULLENBERGER ★

EVEN THE MOST seasoned pilots tip their caps to Captain Chesley Sullenberger III, known to his friends as "Sully," who had both the skill and stones needed to land US Airways Flight 1549 in the Hudson River without losing a single life in the process. But before he became a national hero, Sully spent decades honing his piloting abilities and preparing himself for any harrowing situation.

Born in Denison, Texas, in 1951, Sully spent much of his childhood assembling model planes and watching aircrafts taking off and landing at the airbase near his home. At 16, he began taking lessons with a local flight instructor. A bright student, Sully enrolled at the United States Air Force Academy, where he graduated with the Outstanding Cadet in Airmanship award. After pursuing his master's degree, the young pilot joined the US Air Force in 1973 and became a fighter pilot. He quickly rose in the ranks from flight leader to training officer to captain, leaving the Air Force in 1980 to pursue a career as a commercial pilot with US Airways. He flew thousands of flights over his 29 years of service, for the most part all routine. And then, on January 15, 2009, his gig became anything but.

US Airways Flight 1549 was scheduled to depart from LaGuardia Airport in New

York and land in Charlotte, North Carolina, before continuing on to Seattle. At 3:24 p.m., the Airbus A320 was cleared for takeoff. But less than two minutes after Flight 1549 lifted off from the runway, a flock of dark brown Canada geese swarmed the plane's windshield—Sully instinctively ducked. There was a loud thud, then flames erupted from the engines, followed by an eerie silence. As the smell of burning birds wafted through the cabin, Sully and his co-pilot realized the geese had taken out not one but both engines.

With a fully disabled plane full of people on his hands, Sully radioed air traffic control to plot his next course of action. Could they make it back to LaGuardia? Probably not, he reasoned, concerned about potentially crashing in a heavily populated area. The air traffic controller told Sully he was cleared to land at New Jersey's Teterboro Airport, but after initially saying yes, the captain gauged it wouldn't be feasible, and in a split-second calculation announced, "We're gonna be in the Hudson."

After safely steering the rapidly descending aircraft within hundreds of feet of the George Washington Bridge, Sully uttered his now famous command to his passengers, "Brace for impact." Moments later, the plane hit the water. After working with the flight crew to evacuate passengers onto the wings to await rescue, Sully thoroughly checked the flooded Airbus twice before exiting. Over the course of just 208 seconds, Sully's decades of expertise and calm in the face of danger allowed him to save all 155 people aboard, making for a true "Miracle on the Hudson."

★ SYBIL LUDINGTON ★

TWO YEARS AFTER Paul Revere took his "midnight ride," another patriot jumped on their horse and rode long into the night. On April 26, 1777, 16-year-old Sybil Ludington was thrust into history when a messenger arrived at her house trying to reach her father, Col. Henry Ludington. While her father began to organize the local militia, he sent Sybil to warn others that the British were on the move and fixing for a fight in the town of Danbury, Connecticut, where the local militia had stored their ammunition. Alarmed at the terrible news, Sybil quickly realized the men under her father's command, who were mostly farmers, had already disbanded for planting season. With no time to lose, she leapt on a horse and tore off into the pitch black night to rouse her scattered fellow patriots for the coming battle.

Riding for hours down unfamiliar roads in the pouring rain, soaked and chillled to the bone, the teenager urged her trusty steed onward for 40 miles, stopping at houses along the way to warn their occupants of the approaching threat. Despite her efforts, she could not prevent the British from setting fire to Danbury. But by daybreak, hundreds of soldiers arrived in time to throttle the redcoats as they prepared to leave. Historians are quick to point out that over the course of the evening, young Sybil rode twice as far as the more renowned Paul Revere, and she was thanked by none other than Gen. George Washington for her efforts.

★ JACKIE ROBINSON ★

NO MATTER WHICH major league ballpark you visit on April 15, from New York to Los Angeles, Miami to Seattle and everywhere in between, every player on the field will be wearing the same number. That number is also the only one retired by every single franchise in Major League Baseball, immortalizing it forever as one man's number. The number is 42. The man is Jackie Robinson.

Every April, Jackie Robinson Day reminds fans and professionals alike about the boundless courage it took to be the first person of color to be accepted by the MLB since the pro game was in its infancy.

On August 10, 1883, the Chicago White Stockings, managed by the infamous Cap Anson, took the field in Toledo. When Toledo's catcher, Moses Fleetwood Walker, took the field, Anson became incensed— under no circumstances, he thundered, would his team take the field if Walker was allowed to play. Walker, a black man, was one of just a handful of people of color in pro ball at the time. For Anson, however, even a small amount of diversity was unthinkable. To history's shame, the Toledo club eventually bowed to Anson's rage and before long, the so-called "gentlemen's agreement" to segregate baseball was established.

More than 60 years later, committed Methodist and lifelong baseball obsessive Branch Rickey, working as the General Manager of the Brooklyn Dodgers, decided he was in a position to finally change the racist policy Anson instigated and Major League Baseball had cravenly gone along with for decades. He began an extensive scouting operation of the Negro Leagues, trying to find a player with both the skills to electrify MLB audiences and the demeanor to handle the daunting task of integrating the Major Leagues.

He found his man in Kansas City Monarchs Second Baseman Jackie Robinson. After a stint with the Montreal Royals, the Dodgers' minor league affiliate, Robinson made his big league debut on April 15, 1947. "It was the most eagerly anticipated debut in the annals of the national pastime," baseball historians Robert Lipsyte and Pete Levine wrote. "It represented both the dream and the fear of equal opportunity, and it would change forever the complexion of the game and the attitudes of Americans." Robinson would go on to win Rookie of the Year honors at the end of the season, but his most important contributions came off the field. He played in stadiums where the fans hated him for his color. He played against opponents who were hostile and often abusive. He and his family were constantly threatened. Had Major League Baseball extended into the Deep South in the 1940s, he would have been breaking the law by using the same locker room as his white teammates. But Robinson coolly went about the business of winning games, and hearts, without so much as a raised voice. His courage and grace proved that as the world changed, baseball would have to as well.

★ ROSA PARKS ★

OT ALL PROTESTS involve crowds of people marching in solidarity through city streets, and not all protestors carry signs or megaphones. In the case of Rosa Parks, taking a stand against racial injustice in the Jim Crow South meant taking a seat. Born in 1913, as an African American Alabama native, Parks had grown up steeped in the color-based tensions simmering in the south, attending segregated schools and maintaining a polite deference toward white members of the community, lest she attract the attention of the Ku Klux Klan. But after marrying a man who had been active in the NAACP, Parks soon joined the organization, too, and by the 1950s, the time was ripe for sweeping social change.

On December 1, 1955, while Parks rode a city bus in Montgomery, a bus driver demanded she give up her seat to a white person. "The time had just come," she later remarked, "when I had been pushed as far as I could stand to be pushed, I suppose. I had decided that I would have to know, once and for all, what rights I had as a human being, and a citizen." Rather than comply, the 42-year-old seamstress made the quiet,

bold choice to stay right where she sat, an act which got her arrested. When word of her detainment spread, members of the black community were incensed to know authorities had "messed" with a woman beloved throughout the community for her humble strength—they refused to take public buses for 381 days, and in 1956, the Montgomery Bus Boycott ended with the desegregation of the city's public transit system. Through one simple but wholly profound act, Parks shows us in our own quiet way, we can all be the change we wish to see in the world.

★ IDA LEWIS ★

BORN IN 1842, Ida Lewis was too busy pulling people from the sea and focusing on the day-to-day duties of running a lighthouse to care whether others considered her unladylike for taking on her line of work. When Lewis's father, a lighthouse keeper, suffered a stroke, Lewis was tasked with taking on what had once been his responsibilities: carrying oil to keep Lime Rock Light burning through the night, trimming its wick and clearing the carbon off its Fresnel lens. Living on Lime Rock, a tiny island off the coast of Newport, Rhode Island, also meant that Lewis would have to row her siblings to the mainland in order for them to attend school, which she did without fuss or complaint. But she put her rowing skills to the test as she never had before on March 29, 1869, taking to her boat in the middle of a snowstorm to save two drowning soldiers from perishing in the harbor's icy waters. To thank her for her courage, the U.S. government issued Lewis a Gold Lifesaving Medal—the first woman to ever receive such an honor. Over the course of her 54 years as a lighthouse keeper,

the "Bravest Woman in America" reportedly saved at least 18 lives and made her last recorded rescue at an astonishing 63 years old. When asked to comment on her critics, Lewis simply offered that "none but a donkey would consider it 'un-feminine' to save lives."

John Wayne as Col. Joseph Madden in *Back to Bataan* (1945). With World War II raging in the Pacific during filming, the script had to be updated to reflect new developments abroad.

COL. GEORGE S. ★ CLARKE ★

RELEASED ONLY A few years removed from the World War II battle for which it is named, 1945's *Back to Bataan* is a film so renowned for its truthful depiction it could practically serve as a historical document. This is largely thanks to the film's technical advisor, Col. George S. Clarke, a number of rewrites to the script to ensure accuracy and a star who was completely committed to providing the most patriotic portrayal possible: John Wayne. As technical advisor to the film, Clarke helped create an environment on screen that realistically mirrored the hell of war. In doing so, he helped John Wayne gain a reputation as the best portrayer of the American Serviceman there was.

But that can't hold a candle to the courage he showed throughout his service in the Second World War. As the commanding officer in charge of American military operations on the Philippine island, he was uncharacteristically valiant for one in such a high position, leading the 57th Infantry Regiment of the Philippine Scouts in their fight against Japanese forces. In fact, Clarke was the last man to evacuate the island before it

fell to encroaching enemy troops. After chartering a motorboat and evading roaming Japanese patrols, he boarded a submarine, the USS *Seadragon*, which ferried him to safety at Pearl Harbor.

While Duke's *Back to Bataan* character Col. Joseph Madden is technically fictional, he was based largely on Col. Clarke. Aiding troops in the Philippines against invading Japanese forces, John Wayne's Col. Madden and Anthony Quinn's Capt. Andrés Bonifácio employ complex guerrilla tactics that could have only been highlighted as truthfully as they are with Clarke's expert insight and attention to detail. And perhaps most importantly, *Back to Bataan*'s message to audiences is unmistakable—at the end of the film, Madden tells a Filipino child, "You're the guy we're fighting this war for."

The New York Daily News called *Back to Bataan* "one of the best pictures of the war," and noted that "its realistic presentation gives it an authority that many war films lacked." At a time when American soldiers faced active combat abroad, John Wayne gave a powerfully accurate performance thanks to the authenticity his technical advisor brought to the film.

★ POCAHONTAS ★

WHETHER OR NOT she truly saved an Englishman named John Smith from being executed by her father remains shrouded in mystery, but Pocahontas herself persists as a symbol of the goodwill with which Native Americans first embraced the colonists and explorers who landed in the New World. Born around 1595 to the Chief of the Powhatan tribe, Pocahontas was about 11 when white settlers landed at Jamestown and established a colony. Initially, the Native Americans and colonists—such as John Smith—maintained warm ties. Young Pocahontas worked as a liaison on behalf of her people, accompanying deliveries of goods and mediating occasional conflicts. But as harsh winters and long droughts chipped away at their crops, the starving settlers pressured the put-upon tribes for more and more food, and peaceful relations quickly deteriorated into tense negotiations.

In 1613, the desperate settlers hatched a plan, luring Pocahontas onto a ship and holding her for ransom. While her father acquiesced to her captors' demands, Pocahontas was cared for by a local minister, under whose guidance she learned English, converted to Christianity and took the name Rebecca. Soon after, she married an Englishman named John Rolfe, with whom she had a son. The Virginia Company, the business enterprise behind the founding of the Jamestown colony, looked to Pocahontas as a means to arouse interest in the colonies back in England. Thus, the Rolfes and a dozen Powhatan sailed across the Atlantic on an all-expenses paid trip. But despite her lavish welcome at Whitehall Palace, no amount of royal entertainment could replace the home she missed across the sea. Tragically, as the Rolfes sailed down the Thames en route to America, Pocahontas succumbed to an unknown illness and died. Brave to the end, her generous spirit ensured the survival and growth of the first American colony.

★ TANIA AEBI ★

HEN FERDINAND MAGELLAN first circumnavigated the globe, it was an almost unthinkable feat of navigation, centuries before GPS made civilian sailing on all seas a more attainable goal for the layman. And in 1985, when Tania Aebi set sail on her own circumnavigation, she had many of the same tools to work with. Tania navigated with a sextant and the stars, having taken a correspondence course in celestial navigation before her trip. She had no official training as a sailor, having merely taken a transatlantic trip with her father in a newly purchased boat as a teenager. She fell in love with sailing, however, and between the ages of 18 and 21 Aebi became the youngest person to circumnavigate the globe solo.

Though her feat wasn't recognized by Guinness as a world record because she took along a passenger for a brief 80-mile part of the voyage, Aebi proved that with courage and smarts, a person can find themselves accomplishing the most extraordinary feats.

Despite mechanical issues early in the trip, rough seas and the crippling loneliness of such a journey (broken only by her feline companion, Tarzoon), she persisted in piloting her sloop onward. Her 1989 book, *Maiden Voyage*, about her trip from the East Coast of the U.S. and back, was a bestseller. Upon finishing her two-and-a-half year trip, President Ronald Reagan sent a message conveying his compliments: "You set your energy and youth against an ancient challenge on the ageless seas, and you triumphed."

★ LITTLE ROCK NINE ★

HREE YEARS AFTER the Supreme Court declared that racial segregation in schools was unconstitutional in the landmark *Brown v. Board of Education* ruling, the U.S. still hadn't made much headway with efforts to racially integrate schools in southern states, where segregation had long taken root within the social fabric of the community. This was especially true in Arkansas, where in 1957, nine African American students were denied their right to attend Little Rock Central High School.

On September 4, 1957, Melba Pattillo, Minnijean Brown, Elizabeth Eckford, Ernest Green, Gloria Ray, Carlotta Walls, Thelma Mothershed, Terrence Roberts and Jefferson Thomas arrived on campus to a scene of pure chaos. An angry mob of fuming segregationists surrounded the school, and before its doors stood a line of national guardsmen, guns at the ready. The message was immediately clear: no black students would be entering school. In fact, just the night before, the Governor of Arkansas, Orval Faubus, had called in the Arkansas National Guard in what he claimed was an attempt to keep the peace during the integration process. In reality, he mobilized the Guard to physically block the teenagers from entering the building. Empowered by the support of the local government, the rioting racists spared no insult, hurling slurs and death threats at the helpless students, threatening to lynch them where they stood. This scene repeated itself daily for more

than two weeks, drawing national attention to the South's brazen refusal to abide by constitutional law.

Finally, President Dwight D. Eisenhower could no longer ignore the situation, which stood to challenge his authority as president. (For more about Eisenhower, see page 136.) On September 23, he intervened by issuing Executive order 10730, which allowed him to take control of the Guard and ensure the "Little Rock Nine" could enter their high school without fear of being attacked by violent pro-segregationist protestors. To make sure the people of Arkansas heard his message loud and clear, he sent 1,200 Army paratroopers from the 101st Airborne Division to disperse the riotous crowds who'd threatened to murder the students. With the soldiers Faubus once dared to leverage against the black teenagers now removed from his jurisdiction, the governor could only sit with bated breath as the students were escorted into Little Rock Central High. This infuriated the seething mob, who immediately broke into a frenzy—they threatened to storm the school and remove the students by force. For their own safety, on their first day of classes, the Little Rock Nine were made to leave the school after just three hours. And while the rest of the school year tested each of the teens in various ways, their unwavering courage and grace set a new national precedent in the fight for racial equality. In 1999, President Bill Clinton commemorated the bravery and sacrifice of the Little Rock Nine by presenting the group with a Congressional Gold Medal.

★ DESMOND DOSS ★

HEN THE UNITED States declared war on Japan in 1941, thousands of able-bodied men enlisted in the U.S. Army in an effort to stop the Axis Powers dead in their tracks. As a patriotic American, Desmond Doss wanted to do his part to serve his country. But there was one problem: he refused to hold a gun. Born in 1919, Doss was a committed Seventh-day Adventist, which meant he modeled his life around vegetarianism, nonviolence and abstaining from work on the Sabbath. Through his work at a shipyard in Newport News, Virginia, Doss had been offered a deferment. But he rejected the offer, believing he could still help his country win the war.

Doss's hatred of weapons ran far deeper than his religious beliefs, though. As a child, he'd once watched his drunk father pull a gun on his uncle during a particularly heated argument. Even though his mother had been able to diffuse the situation and grab the pistol before things escalated, when she handed it to Doss and asked him to hide it somewhere, the thoroughly shaken boy resolved to steer clear of guns for good. This traumatic childhood memory, however, mattered nothing to his fellow soldiers when Doss began training to become a combat medic at Fort Jackson in South Carolina.

Angry to find themselves in close quarters with a man who'd entered a war while vowing never to take a life, his fellow Army recruits threw their boots at the conscientious objector in their midst while he prayed by his bed at night. They despised him for being allowed to skip work on Saturdays while their rigorous training and other duties continued unabated. And while Doss insisted he never outright refused military service, no one cared to listen, and he remained friendless as the 77th Infantry Division shipped out to the Pacific theater.

In the spring of 1945, the 77th landed on the island of Okinawa and faced the grueling task of clearing out the Japanese forces encamped atop a formidable jagged cliff. This "Hacksaw Ridge," as the Americans called it, was dotted with caves and holes, making for a particularly arduous climb. When Doss reached the bombed-out plateau at the top of the ridge, with no other means to defend himself, he stayed low to avoid the bullets whizzing overhead, crawling from soldier to soldier. One by one, Doss dragged the wounded to the edge of the cliff, tied them up with rope, then carefully lowered them an agonizing 400 feet to the ground, where they could receive further treatment. Over the course of about 12 hours, he managed to save an astounding 75 lives—including the captain who'd once tried to get Doss transferred out of the unit—without firing a single bullet.

Later that year, for having displayed such selfless valor in combat, Doss became the first non-combatant to be awarded the Medal of Honor.

★ SACAGAWEA ★

I T TAKES A bold spirit to traverse thousands of miles of wilderness on foot. It's especially brave to step up to the challenge without speaking the same language as your traveling companions, let alone if you're the only woman in an all-male group. But Sacagawea faced all of these trials and more as she accompanied William Clark and Meriwether Lewis on their journey to find the fabled Northwest Passage. (For more on the Lewis and Clark expedition, see page 55.)

Born in 1788 to the chief of the Shoshone tribe, as a child, Sacagawea was kidnapped by the Hidatsa, who sold her off to become the wife of a Québecois fur trader, Toussaint Charbonneau. In 1804, when the Corps of Discovery arrived at the Hidatsa villages in present-day South Dakota, they hired Charbonneau to translate for their crew, who brought his wife along for the journey.

Despite being heavily pregnant, Sacagawea fulfilled a number of crucial roles: she spoke Shoshone, which meant she would act as their Native American liaison when bartering with tribes; her presence in the group would highlight the peaceful nature of the expedition; and she would know the lay of the land for a portion of the trip. When Sacagawea gave birth to a son months into their journey, she strapped him into a sling on her back and pressed on. Thanks to the courage and trust of their Shoshone guide, whose memories of her homelands remained sharp even after years of exile, Lewis and Clark traveled safely to the Pacific Ocean and back to Missouri in just two years, maintaining largely peaceful relations with tribes along the way.

★ ASA JENNINGS ★

IN 1915, THE OTTOMAN Empire began purging its lands of all Armenian Christians and other non-Muslim minorities in a brutal campaign of ethnic cleansing. By 1922, the government had killed or deported hundreds of thousands of Armenians. Later that year, the Turkish nationalist army combed the streets of the coastal city of Smyrna for Armenian citizens in hiding; any who were caught were slaughtered on the spot. On September 13, the Turks lit the city on fire, pushing the remaining 500,000 refugees onto a narrow strip of land along the waterfront.

Recently arrived in Smyrna as part of his work with the YMCA was Asa Jennings, a former Methodist minister who'd taken a job with the organization after leaving the church. Horrified by the sight of refugees fleeing for their lives and jumping to their deaths in the sea, Jennings escorted his family to a ship, then turned around and got to work. He bribed an Italian ship captain to take some of the refugees, then secured a flotilla of Greek merchant vessels to ferry people out of the area. Over the course of several days, Jennings's courage in the face of horrific circumstances helped save more than 250,000 lives from certain slaughter by the Ottoman government during the final months of the Armenian genocide.

★ GEORGE WALTERS ★

ON THE MORNING of December 7, 1941, many concerned Americans at Pearl Harbor leapt into action to save the U.S. fleet from a surprise attack by Japanese bombers. One of these brave civilians was George Walters, a crane operator whose equipment stood alongside the dry-docked USS *Pennsylvania*. In fact, Walters had been sitting 50 feet up in his crane when he spotted the oncoming attack. After warning the sailors of the danger at hand, he began swinging his crane back and forth in an attempt to shield the ship from damage.

But because the water had been drained from their dock, the seamen aboard the *Pennsylvania* did not have the same visibility as Walters, making the task of targeting Japanese bombers nearly impossible. To help them, Walters used his crane's boom to point out incoming enemy planes. Rather than save himself by climbing to safety, the gutsy civilian kept up his crucial work, right until a 500-pound bomb exploded on the dock, damaging his crane. But because he'd moved it at the last second, Walters avoided a direct hit. Despite sustaining a concussion, Walters managed to survive the carnage at Pearl Harbor and is credited with helping save the *Pennsylvania* and her crew. Author Walter Lord featured Walters and other largely unsung heroes of the disaster in his 1957 account of the attack, *Day of Infamy*.

★ BESSIE COLEMAN ★

WO YEARS BEFORE Amelia Earhart earned her wings, Bessie Coleman dared to take to the skies as the first woman of African- and Native-American descent to hold a pilot's license. After moving to Chicago to be with her brother in 1916, the 24-year-old future aviatrix found herself working a dead-end job as a manicurist. Before long, she overheard tales of returned World War I pilots and their death-defying feats over the battlefields of France. Intrigued, Coleman looked into taking flying lessons, but as a part-Native American black woman, no aviation school would have her—none of the American ones, anyway. Once Coleman realized she could study in France, she began taking French language classes in preparation for a momentous transatlantic trip.

To her profound relief, the French flying instructors welcomed Coleman with open arms, and just seven months after she arrived in France, Coleman received her international pilot license. Having shown an aptitude for stunt flying and parachuting, Coleman put her daring skills to good use back home as a barnstormer, performing for audiences across the country. For one trick, as a co-pilot manned the controls, Coleman would hop out of the cockpit to stroll along the wings, thrilling the slack-jawed spectators below. Ultimately, she set her sights on opening a flight school for African Americans, but before she could see her lofty goal to fruition, the famed pilot died when her plane crashed on a practice run. Despite being cut short in her prime, Coleman's story continues to inspire people to defy others' expectations in pursuit of their wildest dreams.

★ MARGARET FULLER ★

UNLIKE MOST WOMEN of her time, Margaret Fuller's success in life was largely born out of her father's relentless drive to educate his daughter as rigorously as he would a son. Born in Massachusetts in 1810, by 3-and-a-half, Fuller could read and write; at 5, she began learning Latin. A quick study with a brilliant mind, when Fuller attended school, she found herself intellectually outpacing her classmates. Her fiery confidence, wit and social awkwardness—lessons at home had purposely neglected feminine etiquette—made for a jarring combination, and Fuller's perplexed classmates mistook her unfiltered boldness for arrogance. At 16, Fuller dropped out of school and took to pursuing independent study at home. Free to broaden her academic interests as she pleased, Fuller learned Greek, French, Italian and German, and quickly gained a reputation for being the most well-read person in Massachusetts.

After her father died from cholera in 1835, Fuller took up teaching to support her family and began making friends in the process. In an attempt to pull Fuller out of her slump, they insisted she meet Ralph Waldo Emerson. A former pastor who'd turned away from organized religion, Emerson had recently taken to giving radical lectures on the importance of freeing oneself from the pressures of society. He immediately recognized his newest guest possessed a uniquely keen mind, gaining a lifelong friend whom he soon introduced to others in his transcendentalist circle. Fuller edited and submitted articles for his journal, *The Dial*; when it ceased publication in 1844, she moved to New York to write literary reviews for the *New York Tribune*. The following year, Fuller published her best-known work, *Woman in the Nineteenth Century*, in which she boldly asserted that women and men were intellectual equals and that women ought to emancipate themselves from men by becoming financially independent.

In 1846, at the height of her fame, the *Tribune* sent Fuller on an assignment to Europe, during which she journeyed into Italy to give firsthand reports about how an attempt to establish a Roman republic had resulted in all-out war. During this time, she began compiling a manuscript to document the little-known rebellion against papal rule. Swept up in the fervor of the movement, she fell in love with an Italian revolutionary 10 years her junior and gave birth to a son. As the fighting dragged on, rather than watch helplessly while her lover fought in the streets, Fuller worked to nurse the wounded in a hospital. But when the pope's forces converged on the city in preparation to finish off the revolutionaries in a final stand, Fuller took her family and fled, booking travel on a ship to New York. Sadly, the ship ran aground off Long Island, and all three drowned. One of her greatest admirers, Susan B. Anthony, later credited the fearless trailblazer for having "more influence on the thought of American women than any woman previous to her time."

★ SAMUEL ADAMS ★

A TRUE PATRIOT through and through, much can be said about the fiery Bostonian who urged his fellow colonists to secede from British rule. But it was his total commitment to opposing the Crown at all costs that would define his legacy as one of America's Founding Fathers. As a staunch opponent of taxation without representation, Adams and his second cousin, the future second U.S. president John Adams, formed an underground revolutionary movement. Calling themselves the Sons of Liberty, these daring provocateurs rallied together in secret to incite their countrymen into violent acts of rebellion against pro-British authorities.

After King George III imposed a series of taxes on the fledgling colonies, resentment for the Crown grew to a fever pitch, and when the British passed the Intolerable Acts to punish the colonies for the hundreds of crates of prized tea that had been dumped into Boston Harbor, Adams upped the ante by organizing and leading town meetings to boycott British goods. By 1775, the British-appointed governor of Massachusetts offered a proclamation of leniency to the Sons of Liberty, should they "lay down their arms, and return to the duties of peaceable subjects," with two notable exceptions—John Hancock and Samuel Adams. These two patriots narrowly escaped arrest in Lexington thanks to Paul Revere, who rode out to warn his brothers-in-arms about approaching British forces.

In 1776, after years of urging the colonies to demand their freedom from the reign of the British empire, despite the impossible odds stacked against them, Adams joined with 55 other brave men in effectively signing their own death warrant, the most famous document in American history: the Declaration of Independence.

★ CHARLES BRONSON ★

LONG BEFORE STARRING as the tough-talking antihero in the *Death Wish* (1974) series, Charles Bronson was just trying to make it through his childhood. Born in 1921 to Lithuanian parents in Pennsylvania, Bronson grew up in abject poverty. For want of decent clothing, at 6 years old, the future Hollywood star was forced to wear an older sister's hand-me-down dress to school. By 10, his father had passed away, plunging the family into an even more desperate financial situation, so at 16, Bronson took a job in the coal mines, earning a measly dollar for every ton of coal he shoveled. The dangerous work built up his physique, and the hardscrabble teenager kept at it for eight years until he enlisted with U.S. Army Air Corps. Taunted for his thick accent and limited grasp of English, Bronson brushed off the bullying, grateful to finally have three meals a day.

In World War II, Bronson got the chance to prove his mettle by serving as a tail gunner on a B-29 bomber. Situated in the rear end of the aircraft, tail gunners sat directly in the line of enemy fire and suffered far higher casualties than other airmen. Bravely taking on a post with a short life expectancy, Bronson also overcame struggles with claustrophobia to man the cramped gun turrets, downing several enemy planes over the course of 25 missions. Years later, when he was cast as a claustrophobic World War II prisoner in the 1963 thriller *The Great Escape*, the Purple Heart recipient drew on his harrowing real-life experiences to bring authenticity to the role.

★ EMMA GATEWOOD ★

MANY OF THE heroes featured in this book overcame incredible odds while fighting in wars, designed incredible inventions or pushed the boundaries of human endurance. But we seldom picture heroes as people who survive private hardships, such as those suffering in silence as victims of domestic abuse. Emma Gatewood falls into this second category, yet thanks to her unbreakable spirit, she succeeded in escaping her violent husband to become a living legend on her own terms.

Born in 1887 to a poor farming family, Gatewood was a woman with few prospects. At 19, she married a college-educated teacher who later gave up his classroom duties to become a farmer. He quickly put his young wife to work doing not only household chores but mending fences and mixing cement, and she dutifully obeyed. Sadly, three months into their marriage, Gatewood's husband began beating her. He continued this treatment of his wife for many years, even as she bore him 11 children, and threatened to have her committed to an asylum if she tried to report him or otherwise flee. Bruised and terrified, Gatewood would seek solace by wandering into the woods, drawing peace and strength from her time in the wild. But one day in 1939, Gatewood's husband pummeled her so severely that he broke her teeth and cracked a few of her ribs.

Something in Gatewood snapped— she grabbed a sack of flour and hit back.

However, when a police officer arrived at the scene, he arrested Emma rather than her husband and hauled her off to jail. The next day, when the mayor of their town got a good look at the battered woman sitting meekly in her cell, he took pity on her, bringing her to his own home to convalesce in safety. Not long after, Gatewood's husband left her. In 1941, she was granted a divorce, freeing her of the man who tormented and abused her for decades.

After coming across an article about the Appalachian Trail in a *National Geographic* magazine, Gatewood decided she wanted to give hiking the Trail a try. Despite having no hiking experience, in 1955, she filled a homemade knapsack with a shower curtain, Swiss Army knife, pen, notebook, iodine, Band-Aids and other essentials. In an effort to keep her provisions light, her food supply was limited to Vienna Sausages, raisins and peanuts. She planned to forage the rest, and for everything else, she'd rely on the kindness of strangers, no tent or sleeping bag required.

After setting off at Mount Oglethorpe in Georgia, wearing thin canvas shoes, the 67-year-old hiked an astonishing 2,168 miles alone, crossing 14 states in 146 days before reaching Mount Katahdin in Maine, where reporters stood waiting to interview the smiling "Grandma Gatewood" about her incredible solo trip through the mountains. But none of the overgrown trails or inhospitable terrain could hold a candle to what she'd already endured.

★ VIRGINIA HALL ★

BORN INTO A well-off Baltimore family in 1906, Virginia Hall was the most highly decorated female civilian in World War II. After a hunting accident caused her to lose her left leg below the knee, she learned to use a wooden prosthetic she called "Cuthbert." Around this time, Hall attempted to join the U.S. Foreign Service but was denied entry due to her amputation. After several failed attempts, by 1940, she'd resigned herself to driving ambulances for the French army. But after Paris fell to the Germans later that year, Hall headed for neutral Spain before traveling to London, where she briefed the staff about the German occupation. Here she was recruited by the British Special Operations Executive (SOE), and after surviving night after night of German bombing in the Blitz, Hall fixed her sights on bringing down the Third Reich once and for all.

Back in France, Hall based her operations out of Lyon. She assisted members of the French Résistance in sabotaging German supply lines, helping prisoners of war escape their captors, protecting downed Allied airmen and more. Though "Cuthbert" kept her from being a true gray woman—the Germans referred to her as "the limping lady"—Hall was remarkably good at changing her appearance. According to British author Sonia Purnell, who wrote a biography on Hall, "She could be four different women in the space of an afternoon, with four different code names." As German troops took over Vichy France, the Gestapo chief,

Klaus Barbie, put out a call to capture Hall. Fortunately, Hall had already evaded the infamous "Butcher of Lyon" by dragging herself 50 miles in the dead of winter across the Pyrenees Mountains into Spain.

The American spy didn't linger in Spain for long; she once again departed for London, where she was made an honorary Member of the Order of the British Empire (MBE). Believing she'd been compromised while working in Lyon, the SOE refused to send her back behind enemy lines. Undeterred, Hall asked for a job with the American Office of Strategic Services (OSS), who sent her by boat across the English Channel to Bretagne. To pass as a French farmhand named Marcelle Montagne, she dyed her hair gray, shuffled her feet to hide her limp and even had her teeth fillings changed to match those used in French dentistry. Working on the outskirts of Paris, she organized safe houses, updated her contacts in the Résistance on new developments, relayed German troop movements by radio and found suitable drop zones for supplies in preparation for Operation Overlord.

Following the D-Day landings at Normandy, Hall headed for southern France to facilitate the Allied invasion of Provence. By September, the Allies had turned the tide of the war, and Hall's work was done. For her bravery in fighting the Axis powers at great personal risk, Hall was awarded the Distinguished Service Cross—the only civilian woman to receive the award during WWII—as well as the French Croix de Guerre with Palme.

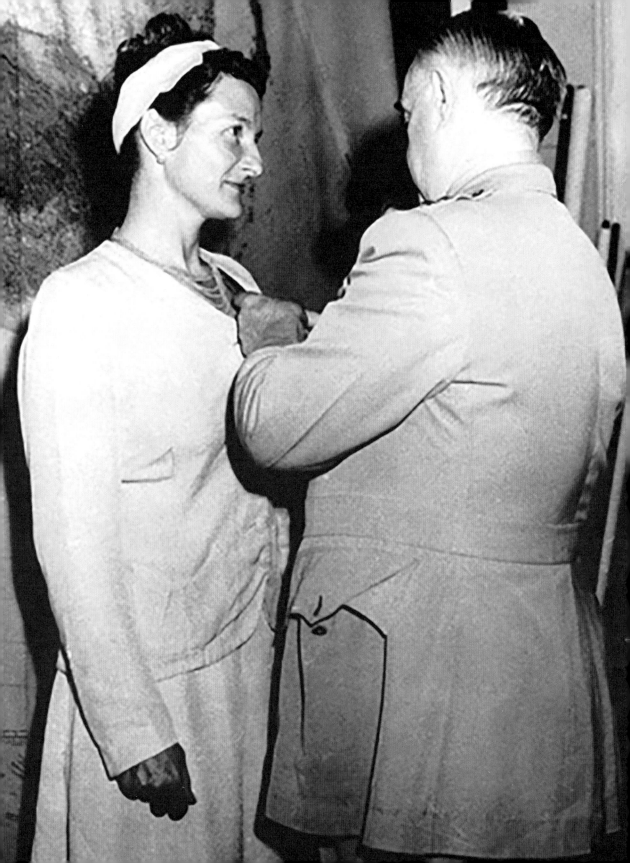

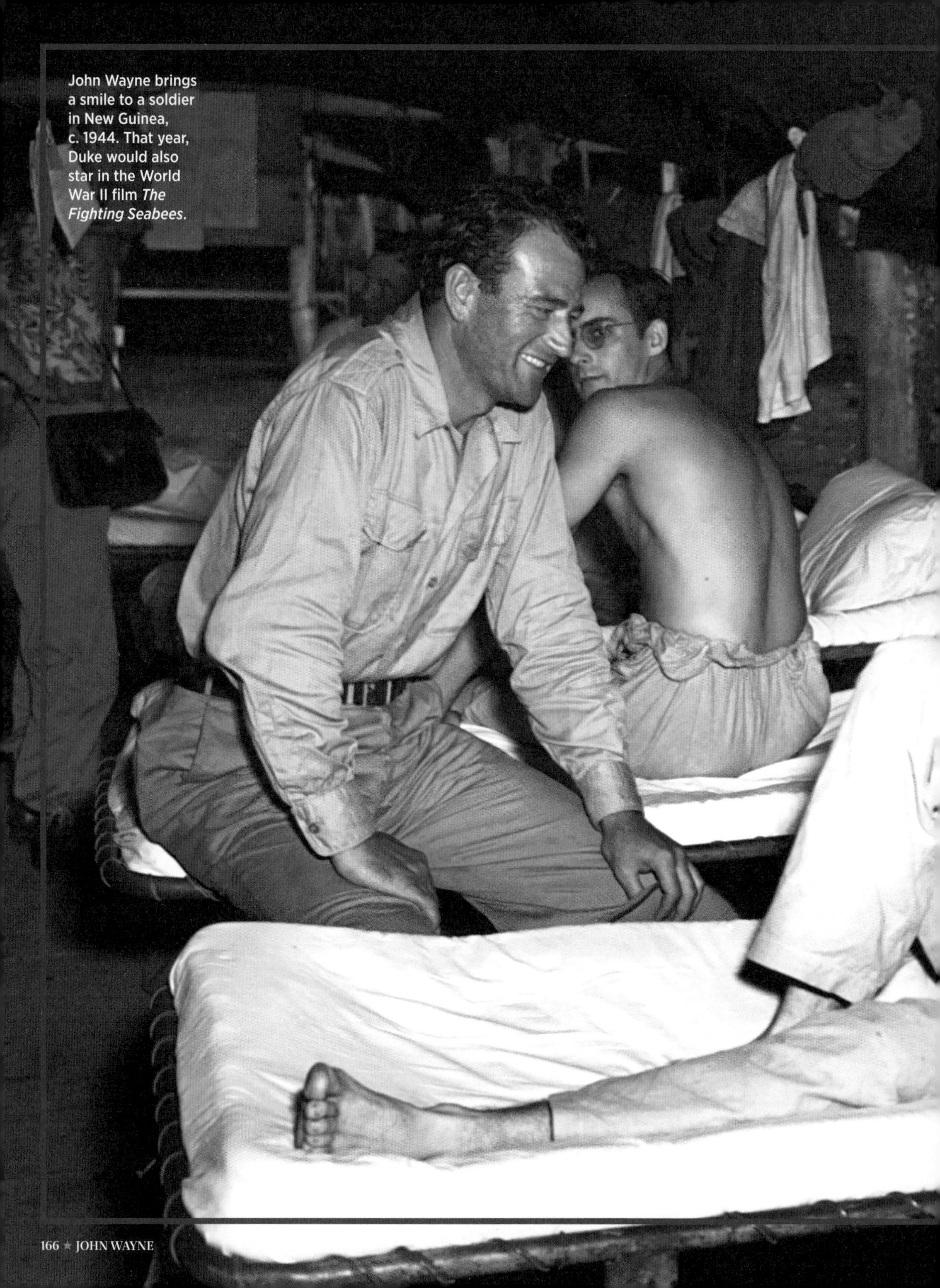

John Wayne brings a smile to a soldier in New Guinea, c. 1944. That year, Duke would also star in the World War II film *The Fighting Seabees*.

★ SACRIFICE ★

SOMETIMES YOU HAVE TO GIVE A LOT OF YOURSELF TO MAKE A LITTLE PROGRESS FOR THE GREATER GOOD.

GIVING HIS ★ TIME ★

AS PART OF A 1943 USO TOUR, JOHN WAYNE DEDICATED THREE MONTHS OF HIS LIFE TO THE MISSION OF LIFTING THE SPIRITS OF AMERICAN TROOPS SERVING IN WORLD WAR II.

NOT LONG AFTER U.S. troops first set foot on foreign ground to defend against the Axis forces of World War II, President Roosevelt mandated a service be put in place to boost the morale of the soldiers giving their lives to the cause. The newly formed United Service Organization—better known as the USO— would quickly respond to this call of duty by creating "Camp Shows," which featured many of the biggest celebrities of the era touring farflung military bases to bring much-needed levity to those in uniform. And among the most fervent supporters of the USO's cause was John Wayne, who worked tirelessly to provide the troops with the comforting feeling of home they had been missing.

John Wayne and musician Vikki Montan greet an unidentified officer during their visit to Australia. A singer and accordion player, Montan was a popular performer in night clubs in the 1940s.

In 1943, shortly after celebrating Christmas with his family, Duke embarked on a three-month tour with the USO that would take him to South West Pacific bases and frontlines across Australia, New Britain and New Guinea. Much like those he hoped to entertain, John Wayne gave his all for a cause he passionately believed in—on each day of the tour, the legend turned in at least two performances. And while that display of endurance alone may seem like going the extra mile, Duke also visited injured troops in hospitals and went out of his way to be personal and approachable to each and every service member he encountered. As the icon later explained in a press conference, taking the time to create connections was the least he could do: "They're where 130 degrees is a cool day, where they scrape flies off, where matches melt in their pockets and daisy-cutter bombs take legs off at the hip. They'll build stages out of old crates, then sit in mud and rain for three hours waiting for someone like me to say, 'Hello, Joe.'"

Of course, being the fearless big screen hero that he was, John Wayne couldn't help himself from being part of the action too. In New Britain, the star met up with his old Glendale pal Fred Stofft, who was serving as a colonel in the war. One day, as Stofft and his men were dealing with Japanese troops who were sending artillery into their area, the colonel went into the head of an aircraft and discovered Duke. "If he'd have been hurt, we'd have been in trouble because he had no business being up in that area anyway," Stofft recalled in a biography.

Still, while he was clearly willing to step outside the bounds of the USO tour's itinerary in order to gain a fuller perspective of the dangers U.S. soldiers were facing, John Wayne was fully aware that the sacrifices he was making to boost their spirits paled in

John Wayne entertains the troops in New Guinea on January 26, 1944.

comparison to those being made by the men in uniform. Nonetheless, Duke's efforts were recognized and appreciated by those who got to spend time with him. Opting to travel to an unfamiliar world far away from his home and his family, John Wayne decided to give up his own comfort in order to provide some to those who desperately needed it. And by choosing to be away from Hollywood for three months at a time when his career was still in its early stages, Duke knew he was potentially

missing out on major opportunities. But the opportunity to bring a slice of America to those sacrificing their lives was one he was not willing to miss.

"These are wonderful guys when the going gets tough," the legend would write in a letter to Hollywood producer Charles Feldman following his USO tour. "It's the greatest thrill and privilege anyone can ever have to see them yell and relax in front of a show." Even after returning to Hollywood, John Wayne continued to be a link to life back home by writing letters to the service members with whom he had formed deep bonds. When speaking to the press about his time on the tour, Duke sustained the idea of bringing America to the troops, and took care to remind the press of the lesser-acknowledged hardship of homesickness that many were facing while stationed across the globe: "What the guys down there need are letters and cigars, more snapshots, phonograph needles and radios... the biggest day in their lives is when the mailman hands them an envelope postmarked 'United States.'"

★ LOUIS ZAMPERINI ★

LOUIS ZAMPERINI WAS born with the will to fight. But like a true rebel without a cause, he had no proper outlet for his pent-up energy until his brother convinced him to join the school track team. As a high school athlete, Zamperini took pride in conditioning his body to run like the wind, a skill that took him all the way to the 1936 Summer Olympics. A few years later, following the Japanese attack at Pearl Harbor, Zamperini heeded the call to serve his country by enlisting in the armed forces. He ultimately joined the U.S. Army Air Corps, where he saw active duty as a bombardier in the Pacific arena.

While participating in a search and rescue mission in 1943, Zamperini's B-24 bomber experienced technical difficulties— it soon lost power, plunging the second lieutenant and his crew into the ocean. Eight crewmen were killed on impact, leaving Zamperini, Francis McNamara and Russell Phillips to fend for themselves on two rubber life rafts in the watery wasteland of the Pacific. The men spent the next month facing blinding sun, scorching heat, agonizing thirst and gnawing hunger. One day, they heard an airplane approaching. Believing help had finally arrived, the castaways watched in horror as the plane opened fire, tearing a volley of holes into their rafts that took eight days to fully repair. Soon sharks began circling them, which the weakened trio pummelled away with their bare hands. They drank rainwater and ate whatever fish and birds they could catch, but after 33 days of living off such meager food, McNamara could no longer hold on; Zamperini and Phillips buried their friend at sea. Two weeks later, the Japanese Navy captured the two starving crewmen as they reached the Marshall Islands, having drifted 2,000 miles over the course of 47 days.

After being taken as prisoners of war, the American crewmen were interrogated, separated and sent to prison camps in Japan. One guard in particular, Japanese corporal Mutsuhiro Watanabe, took a great deal of pleasure in torturing and taunting the emaciated former Olympian, whom he beat almost every day. In one incident, Watanabe forced Zamperini to hoist a six-foot-long piece of wood over his head without faltering, threatening that if Zamperini dropped it, he'd be shot. He held it aloft for a staggering 37 minutes.

Despite malnourishment, exposure, disease and the constant threat of death, Zamperini never stopped fighting and rose to meet each one of his sadistic captor's challenges, including racing other prison guards. In 1945, after two long years of imprisonment, the war finally came to an end and Zamperini regained his freedom. And five years after leaving the camps, Zamperini returned to the country on a new mission: to sacrifice his hatred by forgiving the people who once made his life a living nightmare. Incredibly, the brave veteran paid a visit to a Tokyo prison, where he personally met with some of his former captors who were serving time as war criminals.

Louis Zamperini (right) and Army Capt. Fred Garrett (left) speak with reporters at Hamilton Field, California, following their release from a Japanese prison camp. Zamperini's story was adapted for the silver screen in the 2014 film *Unbroken*.

LT. MICHAEL
★ "MURPH" MURPHY ★

AS THE LEADING member of SEAL Team 10, Navy Lieutenant Michael Murphy had already proven his mettle while serving his country. He'd seen combat in the War in Afghanistan and planned to keep up the fight against terrorist networks to ensure victory for Operation Enduring Freedom. In late June 2005, the 29-year-old led a group of men—Matthew Axelson, Danny Dietz and Marcus Luttrell—on a reconnaissance mission deep into Taliban territory. Their objective: Track down local Taliban leader Ahmad Shah and take him dead or alive.

Code-named Operation Red Wings, the mission initially proceeded as planned: After a helicopter dropped them near the Pakistan border, the men began scouring the remote mountainous Hindu Kush region of Afghanistan, where terrorists and their sympathizers were known to hide out. But just as the SEALs had found a covert place to dig in, a group of Afghan shepherds stumbled onto their position. Startled, Murphy and his men were faced with a difficult choice: they could either kill the civilians, violating the rules of engagement, or let them walk free, at which point the shepherds could alert the Taliban to the SEALs' presence. After a vote, they opted to let the Afghans leave.

Barely an hour later, somewhere between 30 and 40 Taliban insurgents armed with AK-47s and RPG launchers surrounded the team and opened fire. Their special operations mission compromised, Murphy ordered the men to retreat down a rocky slope, but the militants soon followed suit. He then called for backup, exposing himself to enemy fire in the process. Shortly thereafter, a Chinook helicopter arrived, but before it could extract the SEALs, the insurgents blew it out of the sky, killing all 16 personnel onboard. By the end of the firefight, only Luttrell had managed to escape with his life. Because he knowingly put himself in harm's way to make the call to rescue his comrades, Murphy was posthumously awarded the Medal of Honor.

★ DORIS MILLER ★

O N THE MORNING of December 7, 1941, Doris Miller awoke onboard the battleship USS *West Virginia* much as he did every morning, ready to serve his shipmates breakfast before carrying on with the rest of the day's work. This typically involved shining officers' shoes, doing laundry and making beds, but the son of poor black sharecroppers saw it as a vast improvement compared to the limited prospects he faced back home in Waco, Texas.

Just before 8 a.m., the 22-year-old mess attendant heard the alarm to report to his battle station. But when Miller arrived at his designated location, he found it had been flooded; minutes before, a Japanese aircraft dropped an aerial torpedo that blew a hole in the side of the ship, destroying his station in the process. In the chaos, Miller managed to escort his badly wounded captain out of the line of fire. Soon, the ship began to list. With bombs raining down from the sky, it was clear the *West Virginia* would soon sink to the bottom of the harbor.

Miller received an order to assist two officers at a nearby Browning anti-aircraft machine gun. Expecting him to feed ammo into the gun, a senior officer was shocked to see Miller begin pulling the trigger himself, taking aim at the Japanese planes circling low overhead. When oil pouring from the damaged USS *Arizona* caught fire near the *West Virginia*, the sailors found themselves fighting off a barrage of bombs and deadly flames. Despite the massive challenge of being thrown into active duty with zero training, Miller stayed at this post until he was ordered to abandon ship. As one of the last three men to evacuate the doomed vessel, he avoided bullets and blazing patches of oil while swimming more than 300 yards to shore.

For his heroic efforts in going "above and beyond the call of duty" during a time of crisis, Miller became the first African American to receive the Navy Cross. And although he didn' live to see the integration of the armed forces, his actions showed the officers of his day that bravery comes in all colors.

FATHER MYCHAL
★ JUDGE ★

ON THE MORNING of September 11, 2001, many people made the ultimate sacrifice while helping to rescue their fellow Americans. In his capacity as a priest, Mychal Judge numbered in those heroes on that bleak day. Throughout his career, Father Mychal ministered to people who had largely been shunned by society. He provided aid to the homeless, spoke with recovering alcoholics, visited the dying in New York City's first AIDS ward and more. By 1992, he'd been named the chaplain of the New York Fire Department, a position he cherished.

But on that Tuesday morning, when Judge heard planes had struck the World Trade Center, he wasted no time in hurrying across Manhattan to the site.

From left: Father Mychal Judge; firefighter Dan Walker displays a photo of Father Mychal Judge during the St. Patrick's Day Parade in New York City on March 16, 2002.

After meeting and praying for the deceased with Mayor Rudolph Giuliani, the priest made his way to an emergency command post located in the North Tower, where he set to work counseling and providing absolution for the victims and first responders he encountered. But before long, the South Tower collapsed. Debris flew through the lobby of the North Tower, striking him in the head and throwing him clear across the room. Minutes later, as firefighters carried his body away from the tower, they recognized him as one of their own, but it was too late—Judge was pronounced dead at the scene. Of the more than 2,900 people killed that day, he was symbolically declared the first fatality of the 9/11 attacks. When faced with imminent death, the neighborhood priest joined 343 firemen in giving his all to assist the first victims of the worst terrorist attack on American soil.

★ RICK RESCORLA ★

ON THE DARKEST day in American history, Rick Rescorla made the ultimate sacrifice while escorting others to safety. Born in Cornwall, England, he served in the British armed forces before moving to the United States, gaining his U.S. citizenship in 1967 to join the U.S. Army and fight in the Vietnam War. After leaving the military, he transitioned into corporate security. As the head of security for Morgan Stanley on the 44th floor of the South Tower of the World Trade Center, he knew he had a responsibility to protect the thousands of employees in his care. He began examining the buildings for vulnerabilities and discovered a load-bearing column in the unguarded parking garage beneath the World Trade Center. Rescorla alerted the Port Authority to his findings, but the P.A. considered his suggestions too costly and failed to implement his plan. Three years later, in 1993, terrorists detonated a bomb beneath the site, exploiting the building's weakness just as Rescorla feared. Unable to ignore the possibility that the landmark would be targeted for another attack, and after failing to persuade Morgan Stanley to relocate the office outside of Manhattan, he began preparing his fellow employees for the worst by running emergency evacuation drills every three months.

On September 11, 2001, Rescorla was scheduled to testify against the Port Authority for their substandard security measures prior to the 1993 attack. But just after 9 a.m., he felt the impact of the first plane slamming into the South Tower. When the Port Authority (which owned the WTC) made an announcement over the intercom system advising everyone to remain at their desks, Rescorla ignored them. Bullhorn in hand, he marshaled his colleagues toward the nearest staircase and personally oversaw the evacuation of Morgan Stanley's 22-floor office space. Much as he had done in Vietnam, the former platoon leader sang rousing Cornish songs to boost morale and encourage people to keep moving. Tragically, he was last seen going back up into the tower to make sure no one had been left behind. A true American hero, Rescorla's uncanny ability to prepare for the unthinkable saved more than 2,600 lives.

THE FLAG RAISERS
★ OF IWO JIMA ★

T HE MOST FAMOUS photograph of the War in the Pacific and one of the most famous of all American history, Joe Rosenthal's "Raising the Flag on Iwo Jima" came to represent the courage and sacrifice of the American infantryman in a way that would inspire generations. It would also win Rosenthal the Pulitzer Prize and act as the basis for one of John Wayne's most patriotic and best-remembered films, *Sands of Iwo Jima*. It is so iconic an image that it's easy to forget "Raising the Flag on Iwo Jima" represents the likenesses of real American men. They served together in the 5th Marine Division, fought together on the remote island and triumphed together in a moment of timeless victory.

As the United States armed forces pushed toward the heart of the Japanese Empire island by island, the Marines arrived at Iwo Jima on February 19, 1945. Located halfway in-between Japan and the Mariana Islands—where U.S. long-range bombers were kept—Iwo Jima was a small but tactical island whose landscape was dominated by Mount Suribachi, a dormant volcano with a summit about 550

feet above sea level. The island contained three Japanese airfields, which the U.S. Army wanted to use as a strategic point from which to attack the Japanese Home Islands. The Japanese, recognizing this strategic importance, dug in for a particularly dogged defense. Despite the fact that American air superiority and much larger numbers meant victory was all but certain, the Japanese forces made sure that if the island was to be taken, it would be at great cost.

As the battle raged on, it was ordered that an American flag be raised at Mount Suribachi, a statement to the Japanese that the island had been liberated. When that first flag was deemed too small, six marines were sent up the mountain to place a larger flag there, this time for good. Sergeant Michael Strank, Corporal Harlon Block, Private First Class Franklin Sousley, Private First Class Harold Keller, Private First Class Ira Hayes and Private First Class Harold Schultz were chosen for the duty, and thanks to Rosenthal's photo, they achieved immortality in their act of courageous defiance of the determined Japanese soldiers at Iwo Jima.

When the flag went up, the fighting was far from over.

Pfc. Ira Hayes (one of the real-life flag raisers), Navy corpsman John Bradley, John Wayne and Pfc. Rene Gagnon in *Sands of Iwo Jima* (1949).

Newspaper accounts from the days after the battle claim the Marines had to fight their way all the way up to the summit of Mount Suribachi before the full extent of Japanese resistance had exhausted itself, spilling out of tunnels and other hiding places as Marines made their way up. It would be weeks before fighting was over. Tragically three of the six flag raisers would never make it off the island, with Strank—who had refused a promotion just weeks earlier so as not to abandon "his boys" on the front line—Block and Sousley being killed in action.

★ CLARA BARTON ★

WHEN THE SOUTH declared war against the North, self-taught nurse Clara Barton found herself on the front lines of a domestic conflict the likes of which had never been seen. On April 19, 1861, while working at the U.S. Patent Office in Washington, D.C., she encountered members of the 6th Massachusetts Militia who'd been sent to the capitol following a skirmish with a violent mob of Confederate sympathizers in nearby Baltimore, Maryland. A Massachusetts native herself, Barton recognized some of the men and set to work tending their wounds, providing them with food and other supplies. The following year, she applied to work on the front lines, placing ads in local newspapers calling for the public to donate supplies.

The "Angel of the Battlefield" herself experienced a brush with death while lending assistance during the bloody Battle of Antietam, where things got so desperate she resorted to using corn husks as bandages. While helping a wounded soldier sip water, a bullet tore through the sleeve of her dress. It had missed Barton but silenced the soldier in her care. She kept the ripped sleeve as a reminder of the ever-present threat involved in her line of work.

After witnessing soldiers torn apart by cannonfire during the siege at Fort Wagner in Charleston, South Carolina, Barton began organizing field hospitals. And when the war ended, she imparted her hard-earned nursing expertise to freed slaves, embarked on a nationwide lecture circuit along with Frederick Douglass and Ralph Waldo Emerson, and founded the American Red Cross to mobilize aid for victims of natural disasters. Even while struggling with depression from the horrors she saw during the war, Barton risked it all to provide the best quality care possible to those who were willing to sacrifice their lives on the battlefield, no matter their side.

★ RUBY BRADLEY ★

BORN ON DECEMBER 19, 1907, Ruby Bradley knew at an early age that she enjoyed helping others. As a child, the future combat nurse made for a bright student in her one-room schoolhouse and quickly set her sights on joining the U.S. Army Nurse Corps, which she achieved in 1934. Just three weeks after the Japanese attacked the U.S. fleet at Pearl Harbor, the surgical nurse was working at Camp John Hay in the Philippines when Japanese forces took control of the island, capturing the Americans stationed there. Two years later, Bradley was sent to Santo Tomas Internment Camp in Manila. For months, she set about lending her medical expertise to her starving fellow prisoners in their struggle to survive internment. Despite her daily allotted portion of rice—half a cup in the morning and half a cup a night—Bradley saved what she could to give to the children at the camp, and often went without.

As she rapidly lost weight, Bradley's clothes became baggier, allowing her to sneak more food and even surgical equipment into her pockets. Throughout her time in the POW camp, she delivered 13 children and participated in 230 medical operations. Fortunately, on February 3, 1945, U.S. troops liberated the camp. By that time, Bradley weighed a shocking 86 pounds. As she later explained in a 1983 interview with the *Washington Post*, "A lot of people died in the last few months. There were several deaths a day, mostly the older ones, who just couldn't take it."

After enduring three years of captivity, Bradley was sent back home to the states. But rather than retire after such a nightmarish

ordeal, she spent the next few years earning a bachelor's degree in nursing, then shipped off to lend her services in the Korean War. In November 1950, Major Bradley was stationed at the 171st Evacuation Hospital in Pyongyang while the Chinese mounted their counter-offensive. Knowing they would soon be overcome by a massive wave of advancing enemy troops, Bradley saw to it that none in her care were left behind, staying back until she could verify all of the sick and wounded had been loaded safely onto a plane. As Chinese soldiers surrounded the camp, Bradley hopped onto an ambulance and sped to catch the plane as it neared takeoff. The last to board the plane, she turned back to watch a shell explode, blowing her ambulance to bits.

The following year, Bradley was appointed Chief Nurse for the Eighth Army, an opportunity which afforded her the chance to train and supervise more than 500 Army nurses stationed throughout Korea. In 1958 she rose to the rank of Colonel, and after her retirement from serving nearly three decades in the armed forces, Bradley continued her work as a civilian nurse. She was later buried with full military honors in Arlington National Cemetery. To this day, Colonel Bradley remains the most decorated woman in U.S. history.

PRESIDENT
★ JOHN F. KENNEDY ★

BEFORE HE INSPIRED Americans to reach the moon, John F. Kennedy barely survived his childhood. As a toddler, the future 35th president of the United States had already suffered through whooping cough, measles, chicken pox and a month-long hospital stay after contracting scarlet fever, a disease that was then potentially fatal in young children. But as the years passed, Kennedy came to heed his father's words that "when the going gets tough, the tough get going," willing himself through chronic pain. Despite an appendectomy, painful bouts with colitis, a ruptured spinal disk and several more hospitalizations, Kennedy completed his studies and graduated cum laude from Harvard before entering the military.

As a lieutenant in the U.S. Navy, Kennedy was responsible for leading a 12-man crew on a patrol torpedo boat in the South Pacific. Their mission aboard the PT-109 was straightforward: prevent enemy ships from delivering much-needed supplies to their troops.

During the early morning hours of August 2, 1943, while the naval officer and his men searched for Japanese ships, a Japanese warship came into view. But before PT-109 could fire, Kennedy realized the enemy was heading straight for them. Grabbing the controls, he attempted to maneuver out of harm's way, but it was too late: the Japanese destroyer's bow cut the tiny patrol torpedo boat in half and ignited the boat's reserve fuel. While his crew abandoned ship, Kennedy, who'd been violently thrown back on impact, was left to fend for himself. His already weakened back now seriously injured, the naval officer spotted his comrade, Patrick McMahon, struggling with severe burns. Hauling him away from the flames, Kennedy grabbed McMahon before plunging into the sea.

The survivors floated among the wreckage until daybreak, at which point Kennedy— an expert swimmer—rallied his exhausted men to swim three miles to a nearby island. With much effort and in pain, he towed the incapacitated McMahon to shore by clenching a strap from the sailor's life jacket between his teeth. He didn't rest for long, and went back out on another swim to check for American PT boats who frequently patrolled the area.

Over the course of several days, Kennedy and his crew explored a series of small islands to find food and fresh water before eventually encountering two native islanders. The weary naval officer handed them a coconut shell onto which he had carved an emergency message: "NAURO ISL... COMMANDER... NATIVE KNOWS POS'IT... HE CAN PILOT... 11 ALIVE... NEED SMALL BOAT... KENNEDY." By August 8, they were saved.

For displaying remarkable heroism and unwavering determination, the Navy awarded Kennedy the Navy & Marine Corps Medal and a Purple Heart for the injuries he sustained to his back. Long before he led the country from the highest office in the land, Kennedy proved beyond a shadow of a doubt that he would go the extra mile for the people in his care.

★ CAROLE HANSON ★

FOUR YEARS INTO their marriage, Carole Hanson wished her husband Steve good luck as he headed off to fight in the Vietnam War, missing the birth of their first child by just a few months. During his first tour of duty, the Marine Corps helicopter pilot had been lucky, surviving not one but two helicopter crashes. But one day in 1967, a knock came at Carole's door. A chaplain stood waiting outside. "We're not here to tell you that your husband has been killed," he said. "We're here to tell you that he's missing."

Pressing for answers in the coming months wasn't easy—per official policy, the government remained tightlipped about soldiers who'd gone missing in action. But Carole was relentless in her pursuit of information, writing letters to radio stations and embassies, and taking out newspaper ads asking for intel on the status of American soldiers who'd disappeared while fighting abroad. She discovered there were plenty of others like her who needed answers to their own burning questions. With the help of a lawyer, Carole and other POW/MIA wives helped found the National League of Families of America's Prisoners of War and Missing in Action in Southeast Asia. Their emblem: a black-and-white silhouette of Steve Hanson, drawn by Carole herself. The women pressed government officials, celebrities and international figures to help out. Touched by their cause, John Wayne wore a bracelet with Steve's MIA date and penned encouraging notes to her now 8-year-old son with the ending, "Give 'em hell." By 1969, the government changed its policy regarding POW/MIA soldiers. Carole's efforts ensured other military families would no longer suffer in silence, and in 2000, her husband's positively identified remains were interred at Arlington National Cemetery.

President Richard Nixon meets with wives of POWs at the White House on December 12, 1969.

ROBERTO
★ CLEMENTE ★

BORN ON AUGUST 18, 1934, in Carolina, Puerto Rico, Roberto Clemente began playing baseball at a young age. He joined a local amateur league at 16, and just months after he graduated from high school, Clemente signed with the Montreal Royals, the top farm team of the Brooklyn Dodgers. In 1954, the Pittsburgh Pirates chose Clemente as their first round draft pick in the Rule 5 Draft.

As he entered the world of Major League Baseball, Clemente came face-to-face with the ugly realities of racism in the states. More than seven years after the Brooklyn Dodgers broke the color barrier by hiring Jackie Robinson, African American players still faced discrimination and negative press. For Clemente, as a black Latin American still adjusting to life in the states who hadn't yet mastered the nuances of the English language, it was a doubly difficult transition. Rather than print what he said, some journalists took to phonetically rendering his thick Latin accent, injecting broken English into their sports features. When the Pirates traveled to the South, Clemente and other non-white players were made to sit on the bus while their peers dined in restaurants.

Despite these obstacles, Clemente kept his focus on achieving baseball greatness—the 15-time All-Star racked up two World Series championships

and 12 Golden Glove Awards. During the off-season, he focused on philanthropic efforts, and when an earthquake devastated Nicaragua in 1972, Clemente wanted to help. Tragically, he died in a plane crash while flying supplies to victims of the disaster, but his legacy lives on in the Roberto Clemente Award, given each year to upstanding MLB players who best embody the values Clemente held dear.

THE PASSENGERS OF UNITED AIRLINES ★ FLIGHT 93 ★

MANY AMERICANS REMEMBER exactly what they were doing when they first encountered the nightmarish events of September 11, 2001. They can easily recall the image of two planes hitting the North and South Towers of the World Trade Center, of the Twin Towers collapsing in billowing smoke shortly thereafter. Some may also remember the aftermath and wreckage of a third plane crashing into the Pentagon building in Washington, D.C. But the fourth and final plane hijacked that day avoided hitting any national landmarks thanks to the legendary bravery of its passengers.

At 8:42 a.m., United Airlines Flight 93 departed from Newark, New Jersey, en route to San Francisco, California, more than 40 minutes after its original scheduled departure time. Glad to finally be airborne, passengers and flight attendants settled in for the six-hour cross-country trip. Unbeknownst to them, four of the men seated in first class had boarded the plane with knives. Under instructions from the militant Islamic extremist network al-Qaeda, after months of careful planning, they steeled themselves to carry out the final phase of an unthinkable plan.

Just 46 minutes after take-off, the al-Qaeda operatives stormed the cockpit, attacking the captain and first officer before taking a hostage. As the flight approached Cleveland, Ohio, the Cleveland Air Traffic Controllers heard a disturbing message from the cockpit: "Mayday. Hey get out of here. Get out of here. Get out of here." With the flight crew incapacitated, the terrorists succeeded in taking control of the Boeing 757. Immediately, passengers used their cell phones to call loved ones, many learning that the Twin Towers had been hit minutes earlier in New York. Some pieced together that the hijackers were on a suicide mission.

After receiving reports about attacks at the World Trade Center and the Pentagon, the Federal Aviation Administration could not afford to ignore the grim pattern rapidly materializing. At 9:45, the FAA ordered all flights to land at the nearest airport. But when Flight 93 did not respond, officials guessed the worst. Faced with imminent disaster, the only suitable course of action entailed sending fighter jets to down the hijacked commercial airliner, now just 29 minutes outside of Washington, D.C.

As government officials weighed their options, the frightened passengers had voted amongst themselves to fight back against the terrorists who hijacked their plane. After making their last calls to family and friends, by 9:57, passengers and flight attendants banded together to ram a wheeled food cart into the cockpit door. Aware of the revolt happening behind them, the terrorists began pitching and rolling the plane violently, throwing people around the cabin. The plane ultimately crashed in a field outside of Shanksville, Pennsylvania, killing everyone aboard.

While the operatives never named their target in Washington, D.C., whether it was the White House, the Capitol or any number of landmarks, one thing's for sure: the courage displayed aboard United Flight 93 prevented further bloodshed on a day we will never forget.

The Flight 93 National Memorial site in Shanksville, Pennsylvania, hosts an ongoing reforestation effort with the National Park Service and the National Park Foundation to reseed trees in honor of the lives lost aboard Flight 93.

★ THE NAVY SEABEES ★

THE MOTTO EMBROIDERED on the patch logo of the U.S. Navy Construction Battalion—or CB, hence "seabee"—is "Can Do." It's one that every member of the battalion, which started as an extension of the Navy's civil engineering corps during World War I, takes seriously. During World War II, that meant putting their lives on the line to make sure the fighting forces in the Pacific theater had the infrastructure to continue harassing the forces of Imperial Japan. But the Japanese war machine in the islands of the Pacific was so effective the Navy realized as the U.S. entered the conflict that the construction projects necessary to beat the Japanese so close to their home islands would require more manpower and expertise than they'd anticipated.

This scramble for sailors experienced in the building trades meant that most of the first seabees were taken from the ranks of civilian tradesmen who had enlisted following the attacks on Pearl Harbor. They were advanced in rank based on their experience in their respective trades, and the new officer cadre of seabees was born. They weren't career military: they were everyday working Americans, giving the seabees' hierarchy a unique character, which

Duke and his co-stars paid homage to in *The Fighting Seabees* (1944). As they boldly followed their fellow Marines into action to build runways, docks and other essentials under fire from determined Japanese resistance, Duke and his cinematic seabees showed audiences everywhere that not all of the heroes of the war effort were dropping bombs. Some were building, creating new possibilities out of the destruction that surrounded them.

In the aftermath of the war, immediately following the surrender of the Japanese at the Aleutian Islands, the Seabees were among the first warriors of the Cold War. When they were ordered to build an advance station in the USSR, Stalin's government agreed but only gave the seabees 10 days to complete their entire task. The intrepid crew of the U.S. Navy managed to surprise even Stalin's so-called workers' paradise with their productivity. They were also sent to Antarctica in 1946 with explorer Robert Byrd, responsible for

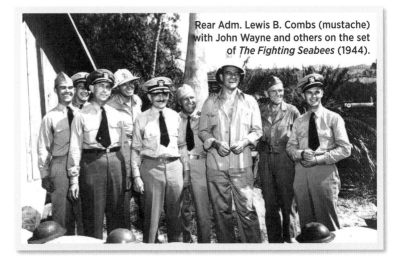

Rear Adm. Lewis B. Combs (mustache) with John Wayne and others on the set of *The Fighting Seabees* (1944).

carrying out classified orders to establish a U.S. foothold in the frozen continent. As the U.S. entered Korea, it was the seabees who built crucial causeways—under enemy fire—that allowed troops to land. They deployed to Vietnam as early as 1954, with the earliest peacekeeping troops. They've also been at the forefront of disaster relief efforts from Hurricane Sandy to the 2004 Indian Ocean tsunami to the Haiti Earthquake and beyond, proving their willingness to sacrifice everything to build what their country needs.

★ THE FOUR CHAPLAINS ★

 N FEBRUARY 3, 1943, the U.S. Army Transport Dorchester was making its way east across the Atlantic en route to an American base in Greenland. Once a luxury liner, the ship had recently been converted to carry troops and other military supplies as part of the war effort and was filled with 902 servicemen, merchant marines and civilians. German submarines were known to patrol these waters, and the crew remained on edge.

Just after midnight, when the Dorchester was about 150 miles away from its destination, a German U-boat spotted the ship and fired. Seconds later, a torpedo struck the Dorchester just under its waterline, killing many instantly and knocking out its power supply. With no means to send a distress signal or sound the alarm to abandon ship, all that was left to do was rally the crew and launch the lifeboats as quickly as possible.

Panic set in. Roused from their sleep by the blast, confused soldiers began screaming and shouting in the pitch black night for life jackets, gloves, anything to brave the freezing waters waiting below. But four Army chaplains (clockwise from top left) remained perfectly calm through the chaos—Lt. Alexander D. Goode, a rabbi; Lt. George L. Fox, a Methodist; Lt. V. Clark Poling, a Dutch Reformed minister; and Lt.

John P. Washington, a Catholic priest—offering prayers, helping the wounded to safety and removing their own life jackets so that others could escape the vessel.

In 20 minutes, the Dorchester disappeared beneath the waves. Of the 902 men that began the journey, only 230 survived. Some claimed to have seen the four clergymen linking arms and praying as the ship disappeared beneath the waves, united in their commitment to give their lives so that others might be saved.

TAMMY ★ DUCKWORTH ★

AS A CHILD growing up in southeast Asia, Tammy Duckworth wanted to serve her country much as her U.S. Marine father had done in World War II. The proud descendant of soldiers who fought in the Revolutionary War originally aimed to go into the foreign service, but after speaking with veterans in her graduate classes at George Washington University, she opted to serve her country as a soldier. With fewer combat role options to choose from than her male peers, Duckworth decided to become a helicopter pilot.

After deploying to Iraq, on November 12, 2004, Iraqi militants launched a rocket-propelled grenade at the Black Hawk helicopter Duckworth was copiloting. It exploded just beneath the cockpit, and as the helicopter spun out of control, Duckworth realized she couldn't work the pedals. Duckworth looked down—the pedals were gone, along with her feet. While her partner took over and managed to land the damaged aircraft, Duckworth lost consciousness and was later evacuated to a hospital in Baghdad, where doctors amputated her legs; in all, she lost nearly her entire right leg and everything below her left knee, and shattered her right arm.

Days after the crash, Duckworth awoke stateside to learn she'd endured more than 20 surgeries, but the fight to regain her health had just begun. The first female double amputee of the Iraq War stayed at Walter Reed (which she gamely referred to as an "amputee petting zoo") for the next year, struggling through grueling physical therapy and another round of surgeries. Over the course of learning how to walk again—this time with prosthetics—Duckworth made the acquaintance of several politicians, including former senator Bob Dole, and in 2005 she received an invitation to attend the State of the Union address by Illinois senator Dick Durbin. Though she cherished her role as a soldier, Duckworth began eyeing elected office as another way she could serve her country.

After forming a friendship with Senator Durbin, Duckworth used her new connection to assist service members at Walter Reed who were struggling with the physical toll of their service and return to civilian life. At Durbin's suggestion, she ran for Congress and lost; but soon after, she was appointed to lead the Illinois Department of Veterans' Affairs, where she created a program for veterans living with post-traumatic stress disorder. Duckworth spent the next few years working to improve veterans services, and by 2012, she'd won a seat in Congress, where she helped pass a bill providing veterans with access to mental health care. Even after giving so much of herself in battle, Senator Duckworth's embodiment of the warrior's credo to never accept defeat is just one of the ways in which she is an American hero.

★ ABRAHAM LINCOLN ★

A NAME SYNONYMOUS with vision, leadership and sacrifice, whole books could be written about our nation's 16th, and arguably most beloved, president. But it was his decision to issue the Emancipation Proclamation that defined both his presidency and legacy as one of our nation's most determined commanders-in-chief. At a time when the country faced its first serious test, Lincoln stood by his convictions as the nation attempted to tear itself asunder. After the Union Army dragged itself to victory over Confederate forces at the bloody battle of Antietam, Lincoln felt it was enough of a win to put his bold plan into action. Clashing with his advisors, some of whom thought it would paint him as a radical, Lincoln was willing to forego the chance of a peaceful reconciliation with the South in order to do what was morally right.

When he issued the Emancipation Proclamation, which declared that all those held in bondage in the Confederacy were free, Lincoln made it clear the Union would have no more arguments of states' rights from Southern states. Human rights would take precedence. It was a simple declaration, but one that constituted nothing less than an all-in bet by Lincoln. The only way to get the South back into the American experiment was through their total surrender. The Union Army finally achieved this at Appomattox in April 1865 after four years of unimaginable sacrifice. Limbs, lives, minds and more had been lost, but the Union's sacrifice was far from through. Mere days after the final surrender of the Confederacy, President Lincoln was assassinated by John Wilkes Booth, who acted as a member of a small cadre of Southern extremists. The Union Army's final, most tragic casualty was its commander-in-chief.

★ HENRY JOHNSON ★

A S THE UNITED States entered World War I, General John J. Pershing made no secret of his belief that black soldiers were inferior to their white peers, so much so that he lent the all-black 369th Infantry Regiment to the French Fourth Army. Among them was Private Henry Johnson, a 25-year-old African-American railroad porter who had given up his job to serve his country on the Western Front. Wearing French military uniforms, the "Harlem Hellfighters" headed for the treacherous western edge of the Argonne Forest.

One night, when Johnson and Private Needham Roberts were on guard duty, German troops began shooting at the sentries. The Americans returned fire, lobbing all of their grenades and releasing a spray of bullets until Johnson's gun jammed. Realizing they were surrounded, he looked over to see a group of enemy soldiers attempting to take the wounded Roberts prisoner. Determined to leave no man behind, Johnson grabbed his last trusty weapon—a bolo knife—and attacked like his life depended on it, clearing a path to drag Roberts to safety. When backup forces arrived, they witnessed the bold private still carving his way through the retreating German troops. The private had sustained 21 wounds in the struggle to save his fellow soldier, but gave as good as he got, killing four and wounding nearly a dozen. For his heroic efforts in combat, the French awarded Johnson their most prized medal, the Croix de Guerre with the Gold Palm for extraordinary valor—the first American of any skin color to win such an honor.

At a time when the armed forces refused them the dignity afforded to their white peers, Johnson and the Harlem Hellfighters showed the nation that no amount of prejudice could keep them from serving honorably in battle.

★ AUDIE MURPHY ★

SMALL BOY who grew up modestly on a sharecropper farm in Texas, Audie Murphy was thrust into adulthood early. After his father abandoned the family, Audie dropped out of school in the fifth grade and went to work picking cotton to support his siblings, of which there were 11.

At 16, Murphy's mother died and he had to stand by as his brothers and sisters were given away to relatives and orphanages. The year was 1942, and America was at war. Despite having lived with more responsibility than many men twice his age, Murphy was too young to enlist—but that didn't stop him. Falsifying his documents to show he was 18, Murphy attempted to enlist in the Marines but they wouldn't take him because he was too short. The paratroopers also rebuffed him. Undeterred, Murphy found placement as part of the basic infantry. It was with this group that Murphy would make his mark on American history.

As a member of the 15th Regiment, 3rd Infantry Division in North Africa, Murphy was thrust into the thick of the German Reich's desperate attempts to stem the tide of Allied invasion. Murphy was with them as they fought their way into Europe, seeing some of his first combat as the Allies liberated Sicily. He was soon promoted to sergeant as he proved his ability to act under pressure with decisiveness and confidence.

By the time the Allies reached Southern France from Italy, Murphy was a staff sergeant with a Bronze Star and Bronze Oak Leaf Cluster for his valor in combat. He was just getting started. As he and his platoon fought their way through a vineyard shortly after landing in France, they were ambushed by German soldiers. Murphy found a machine gun that had been detached from his group and returned fire until the Germans seemed to surrender. When one of his comrades moved to accept the surrender, however, the Germans shot him. Murphy retaliated against this act of treachery by single-handedly storming the house where they were hiding, killing six and taking 11 prisoners. His most heroic action, however, would come in January 1945.

After the Germans hit a U.S. armored vehicle, Murphy had his men retreat into the cover of the woods at the foot of the Vosges Mountains. Murphy himself stayed at his post, firing his rifle at the oncoming Germans while shouting directions on his radio to lead the artillerymen behind him. He mounted the burning wreck of the armored vehicle and used its .50-caliber machine gun to return fire at the Germans, remaining there for an hour and claiming 50 German casualties. For his actions that day, Murphy received the Medal of Honor, and was rightly hailed as one of the war's true heroes. He was also its most decorated soldier.

★ JIMMY STEWART ★

AFTER BECOMING A rising star in Hollywood, James Maitland Stewart put his acting dreams on hold to fight in the greatest conflict of the 20th century. Much like Duke, Stewart put in several years of hard work on his way to stardom. After performing with a summer stock theater company and completing a short stint on Broadway, the Princeton alum scored his first leading film role in the 1936 B-movie action flick *Speed*, during which time he shared an apartment with future leading man Henry Fonda.

But after a series of commercially unsuccessful films, Stewart's breakout role in Frank Capra's romantic comedy *You Can't Take It With You* (1938) delivered the critical acclaim and glowing reviews he deserved. The Academy Award-winning film showcased Stewart's acting chops, positing him as the fresh-faced, earnest boy-next-door antidote to the Clark Gable archetype of rugged macho male leads. The following year, he snagged an Oscar nomination for his spirited performance as the titular hero in *Mr. Smith Goes to Washington*.

But as the Third Reich clawed its way through Europe, the United States began gathering its forces in preparation to enter the fray. A few months before *The Philadelphia Story* (1940) hit theaters, the only film to win him an Academy Award for Best Actor, Stewart received his draft notice. There was just one problem: at 6'3" and 138 pounds, the thin, lanky actor was five pounds short of the minimum weight requirement to enlist. Determined to make the cut, he bulked up with the help of an MGM trainer. After completing his next weigh-in, Stewart entered the Army Air Corps, or what is now referred to as the Air Force.

Following the attack on Pearl Harbor, he narrated two recruitment films, *Fellow Americans* and *Winning Your Wings* (1942), the latter of which the Air Force credited with inspiring a whopping 150,000 men to join the cause. As he already possessed private and commercial pilots licenses, Stewart's interest in aviation served him well during flight training and throughout the course of his 20 bombing missions over German territory.

While conducting one mission over northern France in January 1944, Stewart informed the lead plane of his squadron that they were flying a good 30 degrees off-course, a flight path that would lead the group straight over Luftwaffe airfields. To his frustration, the pilot told him to stay off the radio, but soon enough, more than 60 German bombers swarmed Stewart's squadron and opened fire. Fortunately, all of his men made it safely back to base.

After the war, he returned to the Hollywood scene as a hero, and carved out a wide swath of successful films including *It's a Wonderful Life* (1946), *Rear Window* (1954), *Vertigo* (1958) and *Anatomy of a Murder* (1959). Through this time, he remained in the armed forces on reserve, rising to the esteemed rank of brigadier general, the only actor to ever do so. Later in his career, Stewart joined John Wayne in *The Man Who Shot Liberty Valance* (1962) and co-starred in Duke's final film, *The Shootist* (1976), a fitting sendoff to a lifelong friend.

French General Martial Henri Valin (left) decorates Jimmy Stewart with the Croix de Guerre with palm in France on May 19, 1945. Inset: Stewart and John Wayne in *The Man Who Shot Liberty Valance* (1962).

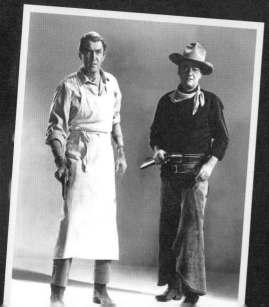

★ ALVIN YORK ★

EFORE ALVIN YORK shipped off to make a name for himself as one of America's toughest warriors in World War I, he was a committed pacifist who'd recently started attending church. When the armed forces denied his claim for conscientious objector status and rejected his subsequent appeal, York found himself heading off to a war he had no desire to fight.

On October 8, 1918, the men of the 82nd Infantry Division faced heavy German machine gun fire. With the enemy on the high ground, the Americans were effectively pinned below. As the situation grew desperate, Corporal York and a group of 12 other soldiers received orders to charge up the hill, breach the German lines and take out the machine guns endlessly peppering their unit with lead. As they mounted their assault, enemy gunfire tore through six troops and wounded three more. While the rest of the group dove for cover, York continued on alone and began sniping the Germans one by one until his rifle ran out of ammo. When six German soldiers ran at York with fixed bayonets, he grabbed his pistol and shot them all dead from a distance.

In his frantic fight to kill the lone American picking his men off like flies, the German First Lieutenant exhausted all of his ammo. Fortunately for him, York took no glory in dealing out justice by the bullet and accepted the German's offer to surrender. In the end, the American sharpshooter was promoted to Sergeant and earned the Medal of Honor for mowing down 25 enemy combatants and capturing 132 more, proving that when you're bold enough to literally stand and fight when no one else will, you deserve to be called a hero.

THE AMERICANS ON
★ THE 15:17 TO PARIS ★

O N AUGUST 21, 2015, three childhood friends boarded a high-speed train from Amsterdam to Paris. Airman 1st Class Spencer Stone, National Guardsman Alek Skarlatos and Anthony Sadler had been enjoying a trip through Europe when Skarlatos heard a gunshot. Stone awoke from his nap to the sound of glass breaking; he looked up to see a shirtless man entering their car wielding an assault rifle and a pistol. Sensing an all-out attack was about to unfold, Stone calculated he had precious seconds to leap into action and subdue the armed man who looked ready to blast through the train.

Stone charged down the aisle and tackled the terrorist, whose AK-47 jammed.

He wrestled and choked the gunman into submission. But when the assailant realized his pistol had jammed as well, he resorted to slashing Stone repeatedly with a box cutter, nearly severing Stone's thumb clear off his hand. As Stone began to bleed, Skarlatos and Sadler rushed to their friend's side, bludgeoning the gunman with his own rifle until he finally lost consciousness. Other passengers stepped in to hold the terrorist down, allowing Skarlatos to take the AK-47 and do a sweep of the train for more potential threats. Fortunately, the friends had contained the threat, saving the lives of 554 passengers. All three received France's Legion of Honour award for their willingness to risk the ultimate sacrifice in order to save those around them.

French honorary consul Guy Michelier and consul general Emmanuel Lebrun-Damiens honor Spencer Stone, Anthony Sadler and Alex Skarlatos at a ceremony in San Francisco, January 31, 2019.

DR. MARTIN ★ LUTHER KING JR. ★

 ONG BEFORE DETAILING his vision for a different America, Martin Luther King, Jr. simply wanted to be allowed to play with his white neighbors. As a young man growing up in Atlanta, Georgia, the future civil rights leader experienced much discrimination on account of the color of his skin. A quick study with an inquiring mind, a 15-year-old King entered the historically black Morehouse College before attending seminary.

Inspired by Gandhi's calls for nonviolent protest, King decided to use his position in the church to enact social change by gathering with other activists in Montgomery, Alabama, where African Americans had recently begun refusing to give up their seats for white people on city buses. A group of ministers and representatives from the National Association for the Advancement of Colored People chose King to lead a city-wide boycott of Montgomery's racially-segregated public transit system. Having only recently been acquainted with Montgomery, they reasoned the young minister hadn't yet drawn the ire of local leaders. Months into the campaign, King's house was bombed. His family survived, shaken but unscathed, and after 13 months, the U.S. Supreme Court upheld the ruling that such segregation was unconstitutional. The boycott had ended in victory.

Two years later, while signing copies of his book about the Montgomery Bus Boycott at an event in Harlem, a woman approached King, asking who he was. After confirming his identity, she thrust a seven-inch letter opener into his chest. Blood pouring from the wound in his collar, King attempted to console his frantic supporters before being rushed to a hospital. A team of two thoracic surgeons spent hours removing the blade, which had missed his aorta by less than an inch. Upon waking, King was told just one sneeze could have finished him off for good.

In the coming years, the Federal Bureau of Investigation closely monitored King's actions and associations with other members of the Southern Christian Leadership Conference. Rumors of communist activity in the group prompted the FBI to wiretap their phones. But despite J. Edgar Hoover's suspicions, King attended the March on Washington, delivering his famous "I Have a Dream" speech before a crowd of 250,000. He and his supporters marched in Selma, Alabama, and faced multiple jailings for participating in sit-in protests. Following the passing of the Civil Rights Act in 1964, King was awarded a Nobel Peace Prize and $54,000, which he donated to the movement he helped lead.

On April 3, 1968, the famous clergyman spoke at a rally for black sanitation workers in Memphis, Tennessee. He referenced his earlier brush with death, telling the crowd, "I, too, am happy that I didn't sneeze. Because if I had sneezed, I wouldn't have been around here in 1960, when students all over the South started sitting-in at lunch counters. If I had sneezed, I wouldn't have been around here in 1961, when we decided to take a ride for freedom and ended segregation in interstate travel." Less than 24 hours later, while standing on the balcony of his hotel, a bullet struck King, fatally wounding him. Despite years of death threats, King never once delayed or postponed his crusade for justice, leading a movement that would carry on long after his passing.

STAFF SGT.
★ MACARIO GARCÍA ★

I N WORLD WAR II, many people felt compelled to do their part in stopping the Nazi war machine from taking over the world. Among them was U.S. Army Staff Sgt. Macario García who, although not technically a U.S. citizen, sought to defend his country in the wake of the Japanese attack at Pearl Harbor.

A native of Mexico, García was three years old when his parents decided to cross the border north to Texas in search of a better way of life. At 22, he enlisted in the Army; two years later, he participated in the D-Day landings in Normandy. On November 27, 1944, the staff sergeant was tasked with taking out a couple of German machine gun nests that had been mercilessly targeting his company. As acting squad leader, García, who'd already been wounded, refused medical treatment—instead, he crawled into battle on his belly to take out the first nest, killing three Germans single-handedly. With little to no cover to shield him, García forged on ahead to storm the second machine gun nest, where he shot another three enemy troops and took four prisoners.

In 1945, García became the first Mexican immigrant to receive the Medal of Honor; and at 27, he became a naturalized citizen of the nation he had long called home. His story serves as a poignant reminder that American heroes aren't born—they're made.

★ CHRIS KYLE ★

HIS FELLOW NAVY SEALS called him "The Legend." His enemies called him "The Devil of Ramadi." But to Chris Kyle, the most lethal sniper in the history of the U.S. military, racking up 160 confirmed kills was just part of the job. Sent to Iraq to protect Marines as part of SEAL Team 3, Kyle shielded servicemen during every major battle of Operation Iraqi Freedom.

On a mission in the Iraqi city of Nasiriya, Kyle faced one of his hardest choices yet when he spied a woman emerging from a house. A small child at her side, she pulled out a hand grenade just as a convoy of Marines closed in. His platoon chief ordered him to take her out. Kyle froze. But when the chief repeated the order, Kyle pulled the trigger and the woman fell to the ground. As

he later reasoned, "The woman was already dead. I was just making sure she didn't take any Marines with her." It was a decision no one should have to make—but Kyle did his duty and protected his brothers in arms.

After four tours in Iraq, Kyle received an honorable discharge from the military but found he missed the camaraderie of the armed forces. Through his own struggles reintegrating into civilian life, Kyle decided to reach out to fellow veterans living with the physical and emotional tolls of serving their country. He penned an autobiography, *American Sniper*, and donated proceeds to the families of two fellow soldiers, and spent much of his time back stateside helping veterans shake the horrors of war. Sadly, the famous SEAL lost his life when a fellow veteran, suffering from PTSD, shot him while the two visited a gun range.

★ JOHN FORD ★

N ADRENALINE-PUMPING, fast-paced action film provides a great source of escape for many moviegoers. In most cases, the directors helming such features have never experienced anything resembling the scenes they craft for the big screen. In the mid-20th century, however, the reality of World War II became inescapable, causing the film industry to adjust accordingly with stories retelling the real-life conflict. But when it came to providing a realistic portrayal of the war, many directors were essentially flying blind. Fortunately, there were also those such as John Ford, whose actual experience in World War II provided audiences an unmatched perspective.

Much like Duke, John Ford had high hopes of attending the U.S. Naval Academy as a young man. But even though he was denied admission in 1914 as World War I was getting underway, Ford would find himself in the Naval reserve decades later as another global conflict was unfolding. Prior to the bombing of Pearl Harbor propelling the United States into the war, the acclaimed director was already petitioning the armed forces to allow him to command a crew of filmmakers who could create effective propaganda. In 1941, Ford's vision was eventually realized as he began leading roughly 30 men as head of the Field Photographic Division.

Within a year of earning his position, John Ford was given an assignment that would allow him to put his talents—as well as his courage—on full display. The Battle of Midway would prove to be among the most decisive naval efforts to take place in the Pacific Theater of World War II, and Ford's filming of the action would forever change his life. While aiming his lens at the historic event, Ford felt the effects of battle after a bomb dropped by a Japanese Zero sent shrapnel into his shoulder and elbow. Despite his wounds, the iconic director continued filming. His efforts would not go unrecognized. Ford later received a Purple Heart and a commendation from the Navy, and the stunning footage he captured would be used in the 18-minute film *The Battle of Midway* (1942), which earned an Oscar for Best Documentary.

When he returned to Hollywood to continue making films in which he could control the action, John Ford was able to operate in a whole new way. Through John Wayne, a man he had mentored since the actor's earliest days in the industry, the director could craft World War II films with unrivaled authenticity. His trust in Duke with the subject matter yielded winning results—but most importantly, the audience knew they could trust Ford to bring an authentic eye to the proceedings. His desire to serve his country in an unconventional way—and at great cost—is as admirable as his skill as a filmmaker.

Director John Ford and John Wayne on the set of *The Wings of Eagles* (1957). During his 1970 Oscar acceptance speech for his role in *True Grit* (1969), Duke referred to his friend and mentor as "Admiral John Ford," noting his Navy rank.

John Wayne poses with sailors aboard the USS *Philippine Sea* during production of *The Wings of Eagles* (1957). The vessel was first launched on September 5, 1945, following the end of World War II.

Media Lab Books
For inquiries, call 646-838-6637
Copyright 2020 Topix Media Lab

Published by Topix Media Lab
14 Wall Street, Suite 4B
New York, NY 10005

Printed in Korea

ISBN-13: 978-1-948174-57-2
ISBN-10: 1-948174-57-X

CEO Tony Romando

Vice President & Publisher Phil Sexton	**Chief Content Officer** Jeff Ashworth
Senior Vice President of Sales & New Markets Tom Mifsud	**Director of Editorial Operations** Courtney Kerrigan
Vice President of Retail Sales & Logistics Linda Greenblatt	**Creative Director** Steven Charny
Director of Finance Vandana Patel	**Photo Director** Dave Weiss
Manufacturing Director Nancy Puskuldjian	**Executive Editor** Tim Baker
Financial Analyst Matthew Quinn	

Brand Marketing & Promotions Assistant Emily McBride

Content Editor Juliana Sharaf
Content Designer Kelsey Payne
Art Director Susan Dazzo
Senior Editor Trevor Courneen
Copy Editor & Fact Checker Tara Sherman

Co-Founders Bob Lee, Tony Romando

Cover: Mantle: Archive PL/Alamy; Iwo Jima: Joe Rosenthal/AP/Pictorial Press/Alamy; Washington: Martin Shields/Alamy; Aldrin: NASA; Background: Shutterstock

Back cover: Salk: Everett Collection/Alamy; Parks: Alpha Historica/Alamy; Roosevelt: RBM Vintage Images/Alamy; Marciano: MARKA/Alamy

2 Photo 12/Alamy; 2 Sueddeutsche Zeitung Photo/Alamy; 2 GL Archive/Alamy; 3 Library of Congress; 3 Photo File/MLB Photos via Getty Images; 3 Everett Collection/Alamy; 4 United Artists/Kobal/Shutterstock; 11 PictureLux/The Hollywood Archive/Alamy; 13 Library of Congress ; 14 Archive Images/Alamy; 15 Science History Images/Alamy; 16 Bettmann/Getty Images; 18 Pictorial Press Ltd/Alamy; 19 Library of Congress; 20 ZUMAPress/Alamy; 23 Vera Anderson/WireImage/Getty Images; 24 Library of Congress; 28 Pictorial Press Ltd/Alamy; 29 Library of Congress; 30 Charles Gorry/AP/Shutterstock; 32 DPA Picture Alliance/Alamy; 33 Visual China Group via Getty Images; 34 Library of Congree; 36 US Army/DoD; 37 PhotoQuest/Getty Images; 39 Library of Congress; 40 IanDagnall Computing/Alamy; 41 Pictorial Press Ltd/Alamy; 43 Library of Congress; 45 Everett Collection Historical/Alamy; 46 Bettmann/Getty Images; 51 Tom Nebbia/Corbis via Getty Images; 53 NASA; 54 Everett Collection Historical/Alamy; 55 Silverfish Press/National Geographic Image Collection/Bridgeman Images; 56 Time Life Pictures/Mansell/The LIFE Picture Collection via Getty Images; 57 IanDagnall Computing/Alamy; 58 Archive PL/Alamy; 60 Library of Congress; 61 Everett Collection Historical/Alamy; 62 Stephen Parker/Alamy; 64 Library of Congress; 65 Album/Alamy; 67 Austrian National Library/Interfoto/Alamy; 68 NASA; 69 Bettmann/Getty Images; 70 Philippe Gras/Alamy; 71 John Olson/The LIFE Images collection/Getty Images; 73 Vera Anderson/WireImage/Getty Images; 74 ITAR-TASS News Agency/Alamy; 76 Owen C. Shaw/Getty Images; 77 GL Archive/Alamy; 78 Wim Wiskerke/Alamy; 80 Hank Walker/The LIFE Picture Collection via Getty Images; 81 NASA; 83 PAINTING/Alamy; 84 GL Archive/Alamy; 86 Everett Collection; 89 Pierluigi Praturlon/Reporters Associati & Archivi/Mondadori Portfolio via Getty Images; 91 Silver Screen Collection/Getty Images; 93 IanDagnall Computing/Alamy; 94 Alpha Stock / Alamy Stock Photo; 95 IanDagnall Computing/Alamy; 96 Evan Hurd/Alamy; 97 Archive Pics/Alamy; 99 Moviestore Collection Ltd/Alamy; 100 GL Archive/Alamy; 101 ZUMAPress/Alamy; 102 Library of Congress; 104 Fotosearch/Getty Images; 105 Archive Photos/Getty Images; 107 Everett Collection; 108 Library of Congress; 110 Hi-Story/Alamy; 111 Look and Learn/Bridgeman Images; 113 Library of Congress; 114 Michael Putland/Getty Images; 115 McCool/Alamy; 116 David L. Ryan/The Boston Globe via Getty Images; 118 Bettmann/Getty Images; 119 Sunset Boulevard/Corbis via Getty Images; 120 AF Archive/Alamy; 122 Glasshouse Images/Alamy; 123 Matt Carr/Getty Images; 125 Lloyd Arnold/Hulton Archive/Getty Images; 126 Batjac Prods/Kobal/Shutterstock; 129 TCD/Prod.DB/Alamy; 131 Warner Brothers/Getty Images; 133 Library of Congress; 134 AP/Shutterstock; 137 NARA; 138 Steve Northup/The LIFE Images Collection via Getty Images/Getty Images; 140 Steven Day/AP/Shutterstock; 143 Mark Rucker/Transcendental Graphics/Getty Images; 144 Alpha Historica/Alamy; 145 Library of Congress; 148 Pictorial Press Ltd/Alamy; 149 Allan Tannenbaum/Getty Images); 150 George Silk/The LIFE Picture Collection via Getty Images; 153 Bettmann/Getty Images; 154 Pictures Now/Alamy; 157 GL Archive/Alamy Stock; 158 Incamerastock/Alamy; 160 IanDagnall Computing/Alamy; 161 Sportsphoto/Alamy; 162 The Denver Post/Getty Images; 165 CIA; 166 Corbis via Getty Images; 171 Courtesy Australian War Memorial; 173 Bettmann/Getty Images; 174 U.S. Navy; 175 U.S. Navy; 176 AF Archive/Alamy; 176 Chad Rachman/AP Images; 179 Joe Rosenthal/AP/Pictorial Press Ltd/Alamy; 180 Library of Congress; 181 PJF Military Collection/Alamy; 183 PJF Military Collection/Alamy; 184 Harvey Georges/AP Images; 185 Photo File/MLB Photos via Getty Images; 186 Maurice Savage/Alamy; 188 U.S. Navy Seabee Museum; 189 U.S. Air Force (4); 191 Brian Cassella/Chicago Tribune/TNS/Alamy; 192 Library of Congress; 193 U.S. Army; 194 Bettmann/Getty Images; 197 AF Archive/Alamy; 197 Keystone-France/Gamma-Rapho via Getty Images; 198 PJF Military Collection/Alamy; 199 Brittany Hosea-Small/AFP via Getty Images; 201 Hulton Archive/Getty Images; 202 NARA; 203 Paul Moseley/Fort Worth Star-Telegram/Tribune News Service via Getty Images; 205 Porges/Ullstein Bild via Getty Images; 206 Everett Collection

JOHN WAYNE
ENTERPRISES

Topix Media Lab would like to thank John Wayne Enterprises, custodian of the John Wayne Archives, for providing unfettered access to their private and personal collection. Best efforts were made by Topix Media Lab to find and credit the photographers.

Topix Media Lab makes no specific claim of ownership of images contained in this publication and is claiming no specific copyright to images used.
The mission of the John Wayne Cancer Foundation is to bring courage, strength and grit to the fight against cancer. www.johnwayne.org